DOCTRINA VITAE PRO NOVA HIEROSOLYMA
EX PRAECEPTIS DECALOGI /
TEACHING FOR THE NEW JERUSALEM
CONCERNING LIFE DRAWN FROM THE TEN
COMMANDMENTS

DOCTRINA VITAE
PRO NOVA HIEROSOLYMA
EX PRAECEPTIS DECALOGI

AB
EMANUEL SWEDENBORG

EDITED BY JOHN ELLIOTT

LONDON
THE SWEDENBORG SOCIETY
2019

TEACHING FOR THE NEW JERUSALEM CONCERNING LIFE DRAWN FROM THE TEN COMMANDMENTS

BY

EMANUEL SWEDENBORG

TRANSLATED BY JOHN ELLIOTT

LONDON
THE SWEDENBORG SOCIETY
2019

Published by the Swedenborg Society
Swedenborg House, 20-21 Bloomsbury Way, London WC1A 2TH

© Swedenborg Society 2019

Cover artwork: Stephen McNeilly
Typeset in Palatino at Swedenborg House
Printed and bound in Great Britain
at TJ International, Padstow

ISBN 978-0-85448-211-5

British Library Cataloguing-in-Publication Data
A catalogue record for this book
is available from the British Library

CONTENTS

Editor and Translator's Introduction	page vii
Abbreviations	ix
Doctrina Vitae pro Nova Hierosolyma ex Praeceptis Decalogi	2
Teaching for the New Jerusalem concerning Life drawn from the Ten Commandments	3
Table of Parallel Passages	123

EDITOR AND TRANSLATOR'S INTRODUCTION

No more than a brief introduction to this two-language edition of **Doctrina Vitae pro Nova Hierosolyma ex Praeceptis Decalogi (VI)** is required. Much that could be mentioned is contained in the Editor and Translator's Introduction to the recently published **Doctrina Novae Hierosolymae de Domino (DD)**, the first of the seven works which Emanuel Swedenborg was seeing through the press in Amsterdam during the second half of 1763 and into the start of 1764. Just the following observations need to be made here in **VI**, the third of 'the Amsterdam Seven'.

Relation to Apocalypis Explicata

The long work **Apocalypsis Explicata (AE)**, which was never completed and therefore never published by Swedenborg himself, includes certain paragraphs, the subject matter of which may be regarded as a forerunner to that dealt with in **VI**. A translation by the late John Chadwick of those paragraphs in **AE** was published by the Swedenborg Society in 1961 under the title **Religion and Life**.[1]

Relation to De Praeceptis Decalogi

A manuscript bearing the short title **De Praeceptis Decalogi (PD)**, which was probably written in 1762 and found among Swedenborg's possessions after his death, is taken to be another forerunner to **VI**. As Norman Ryder states, 'The text of the present MS is not continuous but consists of notes with each topic written on a separate page; Swedenborg evidently used them (with considerable alterations in arrangement) when he composed the work entitled *Doctrina Vitae pro Nova Hierosolyma, ex Praeceptis Decalogi*'.[2] For an edited Latin text of **PD** with English translation, see pages 75-83 of **Small Theological Works and Letters**, published by the Swedenborg Society in 1975.

---

1 See **RB** Volume Three, page 411
2 See **RB** Volume Three, pages 533-535

Other Matters

The placement of Latin text and English translation alongside each other enables readers to identify differences between chapter-and/or-verse numberings of Scripture that were adopted by Swedenborg and those that are generally found in English versions of the Bible.

With the exception of the preference of Swedenborg's printers in Amsterdam for the *ae* diphthong instead of *oe*, his Neo-Latin spellings have been preserved. But his use of capital letters, italics, punctuation, etc., have not been followed, and Roman numerals have been changed to Arabic.

The Divine name consisting of four Hebrew letters which may be transliterated as YHWH or else JHVH, and in most English versions of the Old Testament is translated Lord, is rendered by Swedenborg as **Jehovah** or occasionally **Jehovih**. For more about this, see the Editor and Translator's Introduction to **DD**, page x.

Acknowledgements

Again I wish to record my gratitude to Revd Robert Gill, my consultant, for his continuing close and careful scrutiny of the wording of both Latin text and English translation; to Revd Norman Ryder for his continuing kindness to supply information contained in parts of the **Descriptive Bibliography** which have yet to be published, as well as for his opinions and advice on other matters;[3] to Stephen McNeilly and James Wilson for their continuing readiness to ensure that everything is laid out clearly and artistically; to Judy my wife for her continuing love and presence; and to our Lord for His continuing providential care.

London 2016   *John Elliott*

---

[3] Norman Ryder sadly passed away in July 2018 having submitted the files for volumes four and five of **RB** for publication. These volumes are forthcoming, to be published by the Swedenborg Society

ABBREVIATIONS

Works cited in Editor and Translator's Introduction and footnotes

RB   **A Descriptive Bibliography of the Works of Emanuel Swedenborg (1688-1772)**
edited and compiled by Norman Ryder;
published by the Swedenborg Society
Volume One 2010 (repr. 2017); Volume Two 2012;
Volume Three 2015; Volume Four in preparation

BCP   **Book of Common Prayer**
Edition of 1662 printed by John Bill and Christopher Barker, London

AE   **Apocalypsis Explicata**
Unfinished work, published after Swedenborg's death

AR   **Apocalypsis Revelata**
All editions

AR^1 **Apocalypsis Revelata**
First edition, 1766

AR^2 **Apocalypsis Revelata**
Second edition, 1881, editor Samuel H Worcester

DD   **Doctrina Novae Hierosolymae de Domino**
All editions

NJ   **De Nova Hierosolyma et ejus Doctrina Coelesti**
All editions

VI   **Doctrina Vitae pro Nova Hierosolyma ex Praeceptis Decalogi**
All editions

VI^1 **Doctrina Vitae pro Nova Hierosolyma ex Praeceptis Decalogi**
First edition, 1763

VI^2 **Doctrina Vitae pro Nova Hierosolyma ex Praeceptis Decalogi**
Second edition, 1835, editors L Hofaker and G Werner

VI^3 **Doctrina Vitae pro Nova Hierosolyma ex Praeceptis Decalogi**
Third edition, 1889, editor Samuel H Worcester

VR   **Vera Christiana Religio**
All editions

DOCTRINA VITAE PRO NOVA HIEROSOLYMA
EX PRAECEPTIS DECALOGI /
TEACHING FOR THE NEW JERUSALEM
CONCERNING LIFE DRAWN FROM THE
TEN COMMANDMENTS

Doctrina Vitae
pro Nova Hierosolyma

Quod omnis religio sit vitae, et quod vita ejus sit facere bonum

1   Omnis homo cui est religio scit et agnoscit quod qui bene vivit salvetur, et quod qui male vivit condemnetur. Scit enim et agnoscit quod qui bene vivit bene cogitet, non solum de Deo sed etiam de proximo; non autem qui male vivit. Vita hominis est ejus amor, et quod homo amat, non modo libenter facit sed etiam libenter cogitat. Quod itaque dicatur quod vita sit facere bonum, est quia facere bonum unum agit cum cogitare bonum, quae, si non unum agunt apud hominem, non sunt vitae ejus. Sed haec in sequentibus demonstranda sunt.

2   Quod religio sit vitae et quod vita sit facere bonum, hoc omnis qui legit Verbum videt, et cum legit, agnoscit. In Verbo haec sunt –

Quisquis solverit praeceptorum horum minimum, et docuerit ita **homines**, minimus vocabitur in regno caelorum; qui vero **facit** et docet, hic magnus vocabitur in regno caelorum. Dico vobis, nisi **justitia** vestra abundaverit super Scribarum et Pharisaeorum, non intrabitis in regnum caelorum. Matt.5:19,20.

Omnis arbor quae non **facit fructum bonum** exscinditur et in ignem conjicitur; quare ex **fructibus eorum** cognoscetis illos. Matt.7:19,20.

Non omnis dicens Mihi, Domine, Domine, intrabit in regnum caelorum, sed **faciens voluntatem** Patris Mei qui est in caelis. Matt.7:21.

Multi dicent Mihi in die illo, Domine, Domine, nonne per nomen Tuum prophetavimus, et in nomine Tuo multas virtutes fecimus? Sed tunc confitebor illis, Non novi vos, discedite a Me, **operantes iniquitatem**. Matt.7:22,23.

Omnis qui audit verba Mea et **facit illa**, comparabo viro prudenti qui aedificavit domum suam super petra. At omnis audiens verba Mea et **non faciens illa**, comparabitur viro stulto qui aedificavit domum suam super arena. Matt.7:24,26.

Teaching for the New Jerusalem concerning Life

All religion has to do with life, and that life consists in the doing of what is good

1   Everyone who has any religion knows and accepts that people who lead a good life are saved and those who lead a bad life are damned. For everyone knows and accepts that those who lead a good life hold in mind that which is good, not only in regard to God but also to their neighbour, which is not so in the case of those who lead a bad life. The life in people is their love, and that which they love they not only do willingly but also hold in mind willingly. Here then is the reason for saying that life consists in the doing of what is good, for the doing of what is good takes place in unison with the holding of it in mind. If the two are not acting in unison in a person they are not part of the person's life. But all this must be shown to be so in what follows.

2   All who read the Word can see that religion has to do with life, and that life consists in the doing of what is good, and having read it accept it. In the Word they may find the following –

Whoever relaxes the least of these commandments and teaches people to do the same will be called least in the kingdom of heaven; but the one who does **do** and **teach** them will be called great in the kingdom of heaven. I tell you, unless your **righteousness** exceeds that of Scribes and Pharisees you will not enter the kingdom of heaven. Matt.5:19,20.
Every tree that does not **bear good fruit** is cut down and thrown into the fire. Therefore by **their** fruits you will know them. Matt.7:19,20.
Not everyone who says to Me, Lord, Lord, will enter the kingdom of heaven but those who **do the will** of My Father who is in heaven. Matt.7:21.
Many will say to Me on that day, Lord, Lord, did we not prophesy by Your name, and in Your name do many mighty works? But I will declare to them, I do not know you; depart from Me, you **workers of iniquity.** Matt.7:22,23.
Everyone who hears My words and **does them** I will liken to a wise man who built his house on a rock. But everyone hearing My words and **not doing them** I will liken to a foolish man who built his house on the sand. Matt.7:24,26.

Jesus dixit, Exivit seminans ad seminandum. Semina alia ceciderunt super viam duram, alia in petrosa, alia inter spinas, et alia in terram bonam. Ille qui in terram bonam seminatus, hic est qui Verbum audit et attendit; qui inde **fructum fert et facit**, alius centuplum, alius sexagecuplum, et alius trigecuplum. Cum haec dixit Jesus, exclamabat, dicens, Qui habet aures ad audiendum audiat. Matt. 13:3-9,23.

Venturus est Filius Hominis in gloria Patris Sui, et tunc **reddet unicuique secundum facta ejus**. Matt.16:27.

Auferetur a vobis regnum Dei, et dabitur **genti facienti fructum ejus**. Matt.21:43.

Quando venerit Filius Hominis in gloria Sua, tunc sedebit super throno gloriae. Et dicet ovibus a dextris, Venite, benedicti, et tanquam haereditatem possidete paratum vobis regnum a fundatione mundi; **nam esurivi et dedistis Mihi quod ederem, sitivi et potastis Me, peregrinus fui et collegistis Me, nudus fui et induistis Me, aegrotus fui et visitastis Me, in custodia fui et venistis ad Me**. Tunc respondebunt justi, Quando ita vidimus Te? Sed respondens Rex dicet, Amen dico vobis, In quantum fecistis uni ex fratribus Meis minimis, Mihi fecistis. Et Rex dicet similia ad hircos, qui a sinistris; et quia illi talia non fecerunt, dicet, Discedite a Me, maledicti, in ignem aeternum, paratum diabolo et angelis ejus. Matt.25:31-46.

Facite fructus dignos paenitentia. Jam jam securis ad radicem arborum jacet. Omnis igitur arbor **non faciens fructum bonum**, exscinditur et in ignem conjicitur. Luc.3:8,9.

Jesus dixit, Quid Me vocatis, Domine, Domine, et **non facitis quae dico**? Omnis qui venit ad Me, et audit sermones Meos, et **facit illos**, similis est homini aedificanti domum, et posuit fundamentum super petra. Qui vero audit et non facit, similis est homini aedificanti domum super humo sine fundamento. Luc.6:46-49.

Jesus dixit, Mater Mea et fratres Mei hi sunt qui audiunt verbum Dei et **faciunt illud**. Luc.8:21.

Tunc incipietis stare et pulsare januam, dicentes, Domine, aperi nobis. Sed respondens dicet vobis, Non novi vos unde sitis; **discedite a Me, omnes operarii iniquitatis**. Luc.13:25-27.

Hoc est judicium, quod lux venerit in mundum sed dilexerunt homines magis tenebras quam lucem, **erant** enim **opera eorum mala**. Omnis **qui mala facit** odit lucem ne coarguantur **opera ejus**. Qui autem facit veritatem, venit ad lucem, ut manifestentur opera ejus, quoniam in **Deo facta sunt**. Joh.3:19-21.

34 vobis: illis *VI*

Jesus said, A sower went out to sow. Some seed fell on the pathway, some on rocky ground, some among thorns, and some on good soil. That which was sown on good soil, this is the one who hears the Word and pays attention to it, who therefore **bears fruit and yields**, one a hundredfold, another sixtyfold, and another thirtyfold. When Jesus had said these things He spoke out, saying, Let those hear who have ears to hear. Matt.13:3-9,23.

The Son of Man is going to come in the glory of His Father, and then **He will repay every one according to their deeds.** Matt.16:27.

The kingdom of God will be taken away from you and given to **a nation bearing its fruits.** Matt.21:43.

When the Son of Man comes in His glory, then He will sit on a throne of glory. And He will say to the sheep on His right, Come, blessed ones, inherit the kingdom prepared for you from the foundation of the world; **for I was hungry and you gave Me food to eat, I was thirsty and you gave Me drink, I was a stranger and you took Me in, I was naked and you clothed Me, I was sick and you visited Me, I was in prison and you came to Me.** Then the righteous will answer, When did we see You in such distress? But the King answering will say, Truly I say to you, Insofar as you did it to one of the least of My brothers you did it to Me. And the King will speak in a similar way to the goats who are on His left; and because these did not do those kinds of things He will say, Depart from Me, cursed ones, into eternal fire prepared for the devil and his angels. Matt.25:31-46.

Bear fruits worthy of repentance. Already the axe lies at the root of the trees. Every tree therefore **not bearing good fruit** is cut down and thrown into the fire. Luke 3:8,9.

Jesus said, Why do you call Me, Lord, Lord, and **do not do the things I say?** Everyone who comes to Me and hears My words, and **does them**, is like a person building a house, who laid the foundation upon rock. But one who hears and does not do them is like a person building a house on ground without a foundation. Luke 6:46-49.

Jesus said, My mother and My brothers are those who hear the word of God and **do it.** Luke 8:21.

Then you will begin to stand and knock at the door, saying, Lord, open to us. But He replying will say to you, I do not know where you come from; **depart from Me, all you workers of iniquity.** Luke 13:25-27.

This is the judgment, that light has come into the world but people preferred darkness rather than light, because **their deeds were evil.** All **who perform evil deeds** hate the light for fear that **their deeds** should be exposed. But those who do the truth come to the light, so that their deeds may be clearly seen, because **they have been done in God.** John 3:19-21.

Et exibunt – **qui bona fecerunt,** in resurrectionem vitae, **qui** vero **mala fecerunt** in resurrectionem judicii. Joh.5:29.
Scimus quod peccatores Deus non audiat; sed si quis Deum colit et **voluntatem Ejus facit,** hunc audit. Joh.9:31.
5 Si haec scitis, **beati estis si feceritis illa.** Joh.13:17.
Qui habet praecepta Mea et facit illa, ille est qui amat Me; et Ego amabo illum, et manifestabo illi Me Ipsum; et ad illum veniam, et mansionem apud illum faciam. Qui non amat Me, **verba Mea non servat.** Joh.14:15,21-24.
10 Jesus dixit, Ego sum vitis, et Pater Meus vinitor. Omnem palmitem in Me **non ferentem fructum,** tollit illum; omnem autem palmitem **fructum ferentem,** putabit illum, ut **plus fructus ferat.** Joh.15:1,2.
In hoc glorificatus est Pater Meus, ut **fructum multum feratis,** et reddamini discipuli Mei. Joh.15:8.
15 Vos amici Mei estis, **si feceritis quaecunque mando vobis.** Ego elegi vos, ut **fructum feratis** et **fructus vester maneat.** Joh.15:14,16.
Dominus dixit Johanni, Scribe angelo Ephesinae Ecclesiae, **Novi opera tua.** Habeo contra te, quod charitatem priorem reliqueris; age paenitentiam, et **priora opera fac;** sin vero, movebo candelabrum
20 tuum e loco ejus. Apoc.2:1,2,4,5.
Angelo Ecclesiae Smyrnaeorum scribe, **Novi opera tua.** Apoc.2:8,9.
Angelo Ecclesiae in Pergamo scribe, **Novi opera tua, paenitentiam age.** Apoc.2:12,13,16.
Angelo Ecclesiae in Thyatiris scribe, **Novi opera tua et charitatem;**
25 et **opera tua** posteriora plura primis. Apoc.2:18,19.
Angelo Ecclesiae in Sardibus scribe, **Novi opera tua,** quod nomen habeas quod vivas, sed mortuus es. **Non inveni opera tua perfecta coram Deo, paenitentiam age.** Apoc.3:1-3.
Angelo Ecclesiae quae in Philadelphia scribe, **Novi opera tua.** Apoc.
30 3:7,8.
Angelo Ecclesiae Laodicensium scribe, **Novi opera tua, age paenitentiam.** Apoc.3:14,15,19.
Audivi vocem e caelo dicentem, Scribe, Beati mortui qui in Domino moriuntur a nunc. Dicit Spiritus, Ut requiescant ex laboribus suis;
35 **opera illorum sequuntur cum illis.** Apoc.14:13.

1-2   vitae, qui vero mala fecerunt in resurrectionem *VP³* : *om VP¹, VP²*
6   *om* Mea *VP¹*

And they will come forth – **those who have done good deeds,** into the resurrection of life, but **those who have done evil ones,** into the resurrection of judgment. John 5:29.

We know that God does not listen to sinners, but if anyone worships God and **does His will,** He listens to this person. John 9:31.

If you know these things, **blessed are you if you do them.** John 13:17.

Those who have My commandments and **do them,** they are those who love Me, and I will love them and manifest Myself to them; and I will come to them and make My home[1] with them. Those who do not love Me **do not keep My words.** John 14:15,21-24.

Jesus said, I am the vine and My Father is the vine dresser. Every branch in Me that **does not bear fruit** He takes away; but every branch that does **bear fruit** He prunes, so that **it may bear more fruit.** John 15:1,2.

By this is My Father glorified, that **you bear much fruit** and show yourselves to be My disciples. John 15:8.

You are My friends **if you do whatever things I command you.** I chose you that you **should bear fruit** and that **your fruit should abide.** John 15:14,16.

The Lord said to John, Write to the angel of the Ephesian church, **I know your works.** I have this against you, that you have abandoned the love of others which you had at first. Repent, and **do the works you did at first.** But if not, I will move your lampstand from its place. Rev.2:1,2,4,5.

To the angel of the church of the Smyrnaeans write, **I know your works.** Rev.2:8,9.

To the angel of the church in Pergamum write, **I know your works; repent.** Rev.2:12,13,16.

To the angel of the church in Thyatira write, **I know your works** and **love of others**; and **your last works** are more than the first. Rev.2:18,19.

To the angel of the church in Sardis write, **I know your works,** that you have a name that you are alive, but you are dead. **I have not found your works perfect before God; repent.** Rev.3:1-3.

To the angel of the church in Philadelphia write, **I know your works.** Rev.3:7,8.

To the angel of the church of the Laodiceans write, **I know your works; repent.** Rev.3:14,15,19.

I heard a voice from heaven saying, Write, Blessed are the dead who die in the Lord from now on. So says the Spirit, That they may rest from their labours; **their works follow with them.** Rev.14:13.

---

1   The original Greek here means *We* [ie *the Father and I*] *will come and make Our home*

Liber apertus est, qui est vitae; et judicati sunt mortui, juxta ea quae scripta in libro, **omnes secundum opera illorum**. Apoc. 20:12,13.
Ecce venio cito, et merces Mea Mecum, ut **dem unicuique secundum opus ejus**. Apoc.22:12.

Similiter in Veteri Testamento –

Retribue illis **juxta opus illorum**, et **juxta factum manuum illorum**. Jer.25:14.
Jehovah, cujus oculi aperti sunt super omnes vias hominum, **ad dandum cuivis secundum vias ejus**, et **secundum fructum operum ejus**. Jer.32:19.
Visitabo **secundum vias ejus**, et **opera ejus** retribuam illi. Hos.4:9.
Jehovah **juxta vias nostras, juxta opera nostra** facit nobiscum. Sach.1:6.

Ac multis in locis, quod statuta, mandata, et leges facerent, ut,

Observabitis statuta Mea et judicia Mea, **quae si fecerit homo**, **vivet per illa**. Lev.18:5.
Observabitis omnia statuta Mea et judicia Mea, **ut faciatis illa**. Lev.19:37; 20:8; 22:31.
Benedictiones, si **fecerint praecepta**, et maledictiones si **non fecerint**. Lev.26:4-46.
Mandatum filiis Israelis, ut facerent sibi peniculamentum super alis vestium suarum, ut recordarentur omnium praeceptorum Jehovae, **ut facerent illa**. Num.15:38,39.

Et in mille aliis locis.
   Quod opera sint quae faciunt hominem ecclesiae, et quod salvetur secundum illa, docet etiam Dominus in parabolis, quarum plures involvunt quod qui bona faciunt acceptentur, et qui mala, rejiciantur, ut in parabola de agricolis in vinea, Matt.21:33-44; de ficu quae non dedit fructum, Luc.13:6-9; de talentis et minis cum quibus negotiarentur,

The book was opened, which is the book of life, and the dead were judged by the things written in the book – **all, according to their works**. Rev.20:12,13.
Behold, I am coming quickly, and My reward with Me, **to give to everyone according to their work**. Rev.22:12.

Verses stating things similar to all these may be found in the Old Testament –

Requite them **according to their work**, and **according to the deed of their hands**. Jer.25:14.
Jehovah, whose eyes are open to all the ways of people, **giving to everyone according to their ways**, and **according to the fruit of their works**. Jer.32:19.
I will visit[1] them **according to their ways**, and requite them for **their works**. Hos.4:9.
Jehovah deals with us **according to our ways, according to our works**. Zech.1:6.

And in many other places, where it is written that people were to act in accordance with statutes, rules, and laws, for instance,

You shall observe My statutes and My judgments, **which if people do they will live by them**. Lev.18:5.
You shall observe all My statutes and My judgments, **to do them**. Lev.19:37; 20:8; 22:31.
There would be blessings if they **kept commandments**, curses **if they did not**. Lev.26:4-46.
The children of Israel were commanded to make for themselves a fringe on the hems of garments, so that they would remember all the commandments of Jehovah, **to do them**. Num.15:38,39.

And in a thousand places more.

    The Lord teaches also in His parables that works are what make people members of the church and that they are saved according to their works. Many of those parables hold within them the thought that those who perform good deeds are accepted and those who perform bad ones are rejected, for instance within the parables about the labourers in the vineyard, Matt.21:33-44; the fig tree which did not bear fruit, Luke 13:6-9; the talents and the minas

---

[1] ie come to judge

Matt.25:14-31; Luc.19:13-25: de Samarita qui obligavit vulnera sauciati a latronibus, Luc.10:30-37; de divite et Lazaro, Luc. xvi. 19-31; de decem virginibus, Matt.25:1-12.

3 Quod omnis cui religio est sciat et agnoscat quod qui bene vivit salvetur et qui male vivit condemnetur, est ex conjunctione caeli cum homine, qui ex Verbo novit quod Deus sit, quod caelum et infernum sint, et quod vita post mortem sit. Inde est communis illa perceptio. Quare in doctrina fidei Athanasianae de Trinitate, quae universaliter in Christiano orbe recepta est, etiam hoc, quod in fine ejus dicitur, universaliter receptum est, nempe,

Jesus Christus, qui passus est propter salvationem nostram, ascendit in caelum, et sedet ad dextram Patris Omnipotentis, unde venturus est ad judicandum vivos et mortuos; et **tunc illi, qui bona fecerunt, intrabunt in vitam aeternam, et qui mala fecerunt, in ignem aeternum.**

4 Sunt tamen in ecclesiis Christianis multi qui docent quod sola fides salvet, et non aliquod bonum vitae seu bonum opus. Hi etiam adjiciunt quod non malum vitae seu malum opus condemnet justificatos per solam fidem, quia in Deo et in gratia sunt. Sed mirum est quod tametsi illi talia docent, usque agnoscant, quod fit ex communi perceptione e caelo, quod salventur qui bene vivunt, et condemnentur qui male vivunt. Quod usque agnoscant patet ex Oratione quae in templis – tam in Anglia, quam in Germania, Suecia, et Dania – legitur coram populo qui Sacram Caenam obit. Quod in illis regnis sint qui solam illam fidem docent, notum est. Oratio quae in Anglia legitur coram populo qui sacramentum Caenae obit, est haec –

5 The way and means [to be received as worthy partakers of that holy Table] thereto is: First, to examine your lives and conversations by the rule of God's commandments; and wherein soever ye shall perceive your selves to have offended, either by will, word, or deed, there to bewail your own sinfulness, and to confess your selves to Almighty God, with full purpose of amendment of life. And if ye shall perceive your offences to be such as are not

which servants were to trade with, Matt.25:14-31, Luke 19:13-25; the Samaritan who bound the wounds of the one beaten up by robbers, Luke 10:30-37; the rich man and Lazarus, Luke 16:19-31; the ten virgins, Matt.25:1-12.

3   The origin of the knowledge and acceptance by everyone who has any religion that those who lead a good life are saved and those who lead a bad one are condemned lies in the link between heaven and people who know from the Word about the existence of God, heaven and hell, and the life after death. This link is what gives rise to that general perception. It is why the teaching in the Athanasian Creed concerning the Trinity, which is accepted everywhere in the Christian world, says among concluding words that are also accepted everywhere –

Jesus Christ, who suffered for our salvation, ascended into heaven, and sitteth on the right hand of the Father the Almighty, from whence He shall come to judge the quick and the dead; and **then they who have done good shall go into life everlasting, and they who have done evil into everlasting fire.**

4   There are however many within the Christian churches who teach that faith or belief alone is what saves a person, not anything good done in life, that is, any good work. In addition they say that no performance of evil in life, that is, no evil work, condemns those made righteous through faith alone, because they are in God and in a state of grace. Yet the wonder of it is that although such things are what they teach they nevertheless accept – because of the general perception resulting from the link with heaven – that those who lead a good life are saved and those who lead a bad life are condemned. Their acceptance of this in spite of what they teach is evident from the Exhortation read out in churches – not just in England but also Germany, Sweden, and Denmark – to people attending the Holy Supper. It is well known that these countries contain some who teach faith alone. The Exhortation read out in England to those attending the Sacrament of the Holy Supper is this –

5   The way and means [to be received as worthy partakers of that holy Table] thereto is: First, to examine your lives and conversations by the rule of God's commandments; and wherein soever ye shall perceive your selves to have offended, either by will, word, or deed, there to bewail your own sinfulness, and to confess your selves to Almighty God, with full purpose of amendment of life. And if ye shall perceive your offences to

only against God, but also against your neighbours; then ye shall reconcile your selves unto them, being ready to make restitution and satisfaction according to the uttermost of your powers, for all injuries and wrongs done by you to any other; and being likewise ready to forgive others that have offended you, as ye would have forgiveness of your offences at God's hand: for otherwise the receiving of the holy Communion doth nothing else but increase your damnation. Therefore if any of you be a blasphemer of God, an hinderer or slanderer of his Word, an adulterer, or be in malice, or envy, or in any other grievous crime; Repent you of your sins, or else come not to that holy Table, lest after the taking of that holy Sacrament, the devil enter into you, as he entered into Judas, and fill you full of all iniquities, and bring you to destruction both of body and soul.

6 Haec in Latino sermone ita sunt –

Haec est via et hoc est medium, ut quis fiat dignus particeps Sanctae Caenae: primarium est, ut exploret suae vitae facta et commercia secundum normam praeceptorum Dei; et in quibuscunque animadvertit se offendisse voluntate aut loquela aut facto, tunc deploret vitiosam suam naturam, et confessionem faciat coram omnipotente Deo, cum pleno proposito emendandi vitam. Et si animadvertit offensas tales esse ut non modo sint contra Deum sed etiam contra proximum, tunc reconciliabit se illi, et promptus erit ad restitutionem et satisfactionem ex omni potentia sua, propter injurias et mala alicui facta; et similiter promptus erit ad remittendum aliis offensas, quemadmodum vult ut offensae suae remittantur a Deo, alioquin receptio Sanctae Communionis non facit nisi quam aggravet damnationem. Quapropter si quis vestrum est blasphemator Dei, obtrectator aut sugillator Verbi Ipsius, aut adulter, aut in malitia vel in malevolentia, aut in aliquo alio enormi crimine, paenitentiam a peccatis age; si non, ad Sanctam Caenam ne accedas; alioquin post receptionem ejus diabolus intraturus est in te, sicut intravit in Judam, et impleturus te omni iniquitate, et destructurus et corpus et animam.

7 Datum est interrogare aliquos presbyteros Angliae qui solam fidem confessi sunt et praedicaverunt, quod factum est in mundo spirituali, num quando in templis praelegerunt

be such as are not only against God, but also against your neighbours; then ye shall reconcile your selves unto them, being ready to make restitution and satisfaction according to the uttermost of your powers, for all injuries and wrongs done by you to any other; and being likewise ready to forgive others that have offended you, as ye would have forgiveness of your offences at God's hand: for otherwise the receiving of the holy Communion doth nothing else but increase your damnation. Therefore if any of you be a blasphemer of God, an hinderer or slanderer of his Word, an adulterer, or be in malice, or envy, or in any other grievous crime; Repent you of your sins, or else come not to that holy Table, lest after the taking of that holy Sacrament, the devil enter into you, as he entered into Judas, and fill you full of all iniquities, and bring you to destruction both of body and soul.[1]

6   In Latin it runs –

Haec est via et hoc est medium, ut quis fiat dignus particeps Sanctae Caenae: primarium est, ut exploret suae vitae facta et commercia secundum normam praeceptorum Dei; et in quibuscunque animadvertit se offendisse voluntate aut loquela aut facto, tunc deploret vitiosam suam naturam, et confessionem faciat coram omnipotente Deo, cum pleno proposito emendandi vitam. Et si animadvertit offensas tales esse ut non modo sint contra Deum sed etiam contra proximum, tunc reconciliabit se illi, et promptus erit ad restitutionem et satisfactionem ex omni potentia sua, propter injurias et mala alicui facta; et similiter promptus erit ad remittendum aliis offensas, quemadmodum vult ut offensae suae remittantur a Deo, alioquin receptio Sanctae Communionis non facit nisi quam aggravet damnationem. Quapropter si quis vestrum est blasphemator Dei, obtrectator aut sugillator Verbi Ipsius, aut adulter, aut in malitia vel in malevolentia, aut in aliquo alio enormi crimine, paenitentiam a peccatis age; si non, ad Sanctam Caenam ne accedas; alioquin post receptionem ejus diabolus intraturus est in te, sicut intravit in Judam, et impleturus te omni iniquitate, et destructurus et corpus et animam.

7   I was allowed to talk in the spiritual world to some English clergymen who proclaimed their belief in and spoke in their sermons about faith alone. I asked them whether they believed – when they

---

1   The text of the exhortation here in §5 is transcribed (with a couple of minor modifications of spelling and punctuation) from *The Order for the Administration of the Lords Supper, or Holy Communion* in **BCP** of 1662 printed by John Bill and Christopher Barker, printers to the king, London. See also pages x-xi of the Editor and Translator's Introduction to **Teaching of the New Jerusalem concerning the Lord** published in 2019

illam orationem, in qua non nominatur fides, crediderint quod ita sit, ut, quod si mala faciunt et non paenitentiam agant, diabolus intraturus in illos sicut in Judam et destructurus illorum et corpus et animam. Dixerunt quod in illo statu in quo fuerunt cum praelegerunt orationem, non aliud sciverint et cogitaverint quam quod illa essent ipsa religio, sed quod cum sermones suos seu praedicationes concinnarent et elimarent, non similiter cogitaverint, quia de fide quod esset unicum medium salutis, et de bono vitae quod esset accessorium morale pro bono publico. Sed usque convicti sunt quod etiam illis communis perceptio esset quod qui bene vivit salvetur et qui male vivit condemnetur, et quod haec perceptio illis sit quando non in suo proprio sunt.

8   Quod omnis religio sit vitae, est quia unusquisque post mortem est sua vita, manet enim eadem quae ei fuerat in mundo et non mutatur; mala enim vita in bonam non potest converti, nec bona in malam, quia oppositae sunt et conversio in oppositum est exstinctio. Quare quia oppositae sunt, vita bona vocatur vita, et vita mala vocatur mors. Inde est quod religio sit vitae, et quod vita sit bonum facere. Quod homo sit post mortem qualis ejus vita fuerat in mundo, videatur in opere **De Caelo et Inferno**, n.470-484.

read aloud in churches this exhortation, which contains no mention of faith – the declaration there that if those listening do wicked things but do not repent of them the devil will enter into them as he did into Judas and will destroy them, both body and soul. They said that while in the situation of reading the exhortation aloud they were not aware of or thought anything other than what they were reciting was the essence of religion; but when they were composing and refining the sermons they preached they did not think along the same line, for they were thinking of faith as being the one and only means of salvation, and of doing good in life as being a subsidiary moral duty which contributes to the good of society. Yet they were swayed by the common perception which existed even with them, that people leading a good life are saved and those leading a bad one are condemned, and that this perception exists with them when they are not governed by ideas that are their own.

8   The reason all religion has to do with life is that after death everyone's life is intrinsically theirs, for it remains the same with them as it had been in the world and does not alter. This is so because a bad life cannot be converted into a good one, or good into bad; they are opposites, and conversion into what is opposite amounts to annihilation. Therefore, since they are opposites, a good life is called life and a bad life is called death. Here lies the reason for saying that religion has to do with life, and that life consists in the doing of what is good. As for the nature of people's life after death being what it had been in the world, see the work **Heaven and Hell**, §§470-484.

Quod nemo possit bonum facere, quod bonum est, a se

9   Quod hactenus vix aliquis sciat num bonum quod facit sit a se, vel a Deo, est causa quia ecclesia separavit fidem a charitate, et bonum est charitatis. Homo dat pauperibus, opitulatur egenis, impendit templis et xenodochiis, consulit ecclesiae, patriae, et concivi, sedule invisit templum, tunc devote auscultat et orat, Verbum et libros pietatis legit, et cogitat de salute, et non scit num illa faciat a se vel a Deo. Eadem potest facere ex Deo et potest facere ex se; si illa ex Deo facit, bona sunt, si ex se, non bona sunt. Imo dantur similia bona ex se, quae exstanter mala sunt, ut sunt bona hypocritica, quae deceptoria et fraudulenta.

10   Bona ex Deo et ex se possunt comparari auro. Aurum quod ab intimo aurum, et vocatur aurum obryzum, hoc bonum aurum est; aurum commixtum argento est quoque aurum, sed bonum secundum commixtionem, minus autem aurum commixtum cupro. At aurum arte factum, et simile auro ex colore, non est bonum, non enim substantia auri in eo est. Datur etiam auratum, ut auratum argentum, cuprum, ferrum, stannum, plumbum, tum auratum lignum et auratus lapis, quae superficietenus etiam possunt apparere sicut aurum, sed quia non sunt aurum, aestimantur vel secundum artem, vel secundum pretium aurati, vel secundum pretium auri quod abradi potest. Haec bonitate differunt ab ipso auro, sicut vestis ab homine. Potest etiam lignum putidum et scoria, imo fimus, induci auro; hoc aurum est quod cum bono Pharisaico comparabile est.

11   Homo ex scientia novit num aurum in substantia bonum est, num commixtum et falsificatum, et num inductum, sed non ex scientia novit num bonum quod facit in se bonum est. Hoc solum novit, quod bonum a Deo bonum sit et quod

None can from themselves do anything good that is truly good

9   Till now scarcely anyone has known whether the good they do springs from self or from God, for the reason that the church has separated faith from charity or the love of others, and goodness pertains to the love of others. People give to the poor, help those in need, endow places of worship and hospitals, contribute to the welfare of church, country, and fellow citizen, enter with respect a place of worship and then listen and pray devoutly, read the Word and books of spirituality, and think about salvation, yet they do not know whether these things they do spring from self or from God. The same deeds people perform can spring from God or they can spring from self; if they do so from God they are good, if from self they are not good. Indeed there are some deeds resembling those that are good which are obviously bad, such as the good deeds performed by a hypocrite, which are deceiving and fraudulent.

10   Forms of goodness springing from God and from self may be likened to gold. Gold that is gold all through, called fine gold, is good gold; gold alloyed with silver is also gold, but good only to the extent it is present in the alloy; gold alloyed with copper however is good even less so. But gold that is artificial, and gold-like in colour, is not good because there is no actual gold in it. There is also that which is gilded, such as gilded silver, copper, iron, tin, or lead, as well as gilded wood and stone, which superficially may look like gold, but because they are not gold are valued according to artistic merit, the price of what is gilt, or the price of the gold that can be peeled off. These are different in goodness from real gold, just as a garment is different from the person wearing it. It is also possible for rotten wood and drossy metal, even excrement, to be overlaid with gold. This gold may be likened to the good performed by Pharisees.

11   Worldly knowledge enables people to know whether gold is wholly good, or alloyed and counterfeit, or gilt, but it does not enable them to know whether the good they do is truly good. Only this do they know, that good springing from God is good and good springing

bonum ab homine non bonum sit. Quare quia interest saluti scire num bonum quod facit a Deo sit vel num a Deo non sit, ideo revelandum est; sed antequam revelatur, dicetur aliquid de bonis.

12   Datur bonum civile, bonum morale, et bonum spirituale. Bonum civile est quod homo facit ex lege civili; per id bonum et secundum id est homo civis in mundo naturali. Bonum morale est quod homo facit ex lege rationali; per id bonum et secundum id est ille homo. Bonum spirituale est quod homo facit ex lege spirituali; per id bonum et secundum id est homo civis in mundo spirituali. Haec bona sequuntur in hoc ordine: bonum spirituale est supremum, bonum morale est medium, et bonum civile est ultimum.

13   Homo cui est bonum spirituale est homo moralis et quoque homo civilis, at homo cui non est bonum spirituale apparet sicut sit homo moralis et civilis, sed usque non est. Quod homo cui est bonum spirituale sit homo moralis et civilis, est quia bonum spirituale essentiam boni in se habet, et ex illo bonum morale et civile. Essentia boni non potest dari aliunde quam ab Ipso qui est ipsum bonum. Effunde cogitationem quaquaversum, intende, et inquire unde bonum est bonum, et videbis quod sit a suo esse, et quod id sit bonum quod esse boni in se habet, consequenter quod id sit bonum quod est ab ipso bono, ita a Deo; consequenter quod bonum non a Deo sed ab homine non bonum sit.

14   Ex illis quae in **Doctrina de Scriptura Sacra**, n.27,28,38, dicta sunt, videri potest quod supremum, medium, et ultimum faciant unum, sicut finis, causa, et effectus; et quod quia faciunt unum, ipse finis dicatur finis primus, causa finis medius, et effectus finis ultimus. Inde patebit quod apud hominem cui bonum spirituale est, morale apud illum sit spirituale medium, ac quod civile sit spirituale ultimum. Inde nunc est quod dictum sit quod homo cui est bonum spirituale sit homo moralis et homo civilis, et quod homo cui non est bonum spirituale non sit homo moralis, nec civilis, sed quod modo appareat sicut sit. Apparet sibi et quoque aliis.

from a person is not good. Therefore, because it is important for their salvation for people to know whether the good they do springs from God or not from God, this is a matter that needs to be revealed. But before that something must be said about kinds of good.

12   There is civic good, moral good, and spiritual good. Civic good is that which people perform in accord with the law of the city or state they belong to; this good is what makes them and determines how far they are proper citizens in the natural world. Moral good is that which people perform in accord with the law of reason; this good is what makes them and determines how far they are proper human beings. Spiritual good is that which people perform in accord with spiritual law; this good is what makes and determines how far they are proper citizens in the spiritual world. These kinds of good follow one another in this order: spiritual good is highest, moral good comes in the middle, and civic good stands last and lowest.

13   People who perform spiritual good are moral people and also proper citizens, but those who do not perform spiritual good can appear to be moral and proper citizens, but are nevertheless not so. The reason why those who perform spiritual good are moral and proper citizens as well is that spiritual good is absolutely good, and from it moral and civic good flow. That which is absolutely good can spring from no other source than Him who is goodness itself. Turn and focus your mind in any direction whatever, and ask from where does goodness get its goodness. You will recognize that it does so from its own inner being, and that that is good which has the very being of goodness within it, consequently that is good which springs from goodness itself, thus from God; and consequently that good which does not spring from God but has a human origin is not good.

14   From what has been stated in §§27,28,38 of **Teaching concerning Sacred Scripture**, it may be seen that what is the highest level, what is the middle, and what the last or lowest make one, as do end in view, cause, and effect; and that because they make one, the end in view is called the first or primary end, the cause the middle end, and the effect the last and lowest end. From all this it will be evident that with people whose goodness is spiritual, morality with them is the middle level of their spiritual goodness, and citizenship the last and lowest. This then is the reason for stating that people whose goodness is spiritual are moral people and proper citizens, and that those who have no spiritual goodness are not moral people, nor are they proper citizens, but merely appear to be so. They appear so to themselves as well as to others.

15 Quod homo qui non spiritualis est usque possit rationaliter cogitare et inde loqui, sicut spiritualis homo, est quia intellectus hominis potest elevari in lucem caeli, quae est veritas, et ex illa videre; sed voluntas hominis non potest similiter elevari in calorem caeli, qui est amor, et ex illo facere. Inde est quod veritas et amor non unum faciant apud hominem nisi spiritualis sit. Inde etiam est quod homo possit loqui; hoc etiam facit discrimen inter hominem et inter bestiam. Per hoc quod intellectus possit elevari in caelum, cum adhuc non voluntas, est quod homo possit reformari et spiritualis fieri, sed tunc primum reformatur et spiritualis fit, quando etiam voluntas elevatur. Ex illa dote intellectus prae dote voluntatis, est quod homo, qualiscunque sit, etiam malus, possit rationaliter cogitare et inde loqui, sicut spiritualis. Sed quod non usque rationalis sit, est quia intellectus non ducit voluntatem, sed voluntas intellectum. Intellectus modo docet et monstrat viam, ut in **Doctrina de Scriptura Sacra**, n.115, dictum est, et quamdiu voluntas non una cum intellectu est in caelo, homo non est spiritualis, et inde nec rationalis; nam cum relinquitur suae voluntati seu suo amori, tunc rationalia intellectus sui de Deo, de caelo, et de vita aeterna, ejicit, et loco illorum assumit talia quae cum voluntatis ejus amore concordant, et illa vocat rationalia. Sed haec videnda erunt in transactionibus de **Sapientia Angelica**.

16 In sequentibus illi qui bonum faciunt a se dicentur homines naturales, quoniam morale et civile apud illos quoad essentiam est naturale. At illi qui bonum faciunt a Domino dicentur homines spirituales, quoniam morale et civile apud illos quoad essentiam est spirituale.

17 Quod nemo possit facere aliquod bonum quod bonum est, a se, docet Dominus apud Johannem,

Homo non potest sumere quicquam nisi sit datum illi e caelo. 3:27.

Et apud eundem,

15   People who are not spiritual are nevertheless able to think and consequently speak rationally, just the same as those who are spiritual. They can do so because the human understanding is able to be raised into the light of heaven, which is the truth present there, and to see things in that light; but the human will is not able to be raised in a similar way into the warmth of heaven, that is, the love existing there, and to act under the influence of this warmth. One consequence of all this is that truth and love do not make one with a person unless the person is spiritual. But another consequence is that human beings possess the power of speech, which also makes them different from animals. This capability of the understanding to be raised up to heaven, though not yet the will as well, is what enables a person to be reformed and become spiritual; but as soon as the person is reformed and becomes spiritual the will is raised too. This power of the understanding rather than that of the will is what allows people – whatever their character may be, even wicked – to think and consequently speak rationally, just the same as those who are spiritual. Yet they are not rational, because their understanding does not lead their will; instead will leads understanding. The role of the understanding is to inform and show the way, as stated in **Teaching concerning Sacred Scripture**, §115; and for as long as their will does not go together with the understanding in heaven people are not spiritual, and not therefore rational either. For when left to themselves – to the will or love that is their own – they cast aside the rational concepts, present in their understanding, of God, heaven, and eternal life, and in place of these take hold of the sorts of ideas that concur with the love belonging to their will and call these ideas rational instead. But more on these matters will be seen among the subjects to be dealt with regarding **Angelic Wisdom**.[1]

16   In what follows, those who from themselves do what is good will be called natural people, because with them the whole nature of that which is moral and civic is natural. Those however who from the Lord do what is good will be called spiritual people, because with them the whole nature of that which is moral and civic is spiritual.

17   None are able from self to do anything good that is truly good; this is the Lord's teaching in John,

People cannot receive anything unless it is given them from heaven. 3:27.

And in the same gospel,

   1   See – in the author's Preface to **Teaching of the New Jerusalem concerning the Lord** – the last four on the nine subjects Swedenborg was intending to deal with in forthcoming publications

Qui manet in Me et Ego in illo, hic fert fructum multum, quia sine Me non potestis facere quicquam. 15:5.

Qui manet in Me et Ego in illo, hic fert fructum multum, est quod a Domino sit omne bonum; fructus est bonum. Sine Me non potestis facere quicquam, est quod nemo id possit facere a se. Illi qui credunt in Dominum, et bonum faciunt ab Ipso, vocantur Filii lucis, Joh.12:36; Luc.16:8; Filii nuptiarum, Marc.2:19; Filii resurrectionis, Luc.20:36; Filii Dei, Luc.20:36; Joh.1:12; Ex Deo nati, Joh.1:13; quod Deum visuri sint, Matt.5:8; quod Dominus mansionem apud illos facturus sit, Joh.14:23; quod fidem Dei habeant, Marc.11:22; quod opera illorum sint a Deo facta, Joh.3:21. Haec in summa sunt in his verbis,

Quotquot receperunt Ipsum, dedit illis potestatem ut filii Dei essent, credentibus in nomen Ipsius, qui non ex sanguinibus, neque e voluntate carnis, neque e voluntate viri, sed ex Deo nati sunt. Joh.1:12,13.

Credere in nomen Filii Dei est credere Verbum et vivere secundum id; voluntas carnis est proprium voluntatis hominis, quod in se est malum, et voluntas viri est proprium intellectus ejus, quod in se est falsum ex malo; nati ex illis sunt qui ex proprio volunt et faciunt, ac cogitant et loquuntur, nati a Deo sunt qui illa ex Domino. In summa, quod non bonum sit quod ab homine sed quod bonum sit quod a Domino.

13 Ipsum: Jesum *VI*

Those who abide in Me, and I in them, they it is who bear much fruit, for without Me you can do nothing. 15:5.

These words – Those who abide in Me and I in them, they it is who bear much fruit – mean that the Lord is the source of all that is good, fruit being that which is good. And the words – Without Me you can do nothing – mean that from self none are able to do so. Those who believe in the Lord and from Him do what is good are called Children of light, John 12:36; Luke 16:8; Children of the wedding,[1] Mark 2:19; Children of the resurrection, Luke 20:36; Children of God, Luke 20:36; John 1:12; Born of God, John 1:13. It is said in reference to them that they will see God, Matt.5:8; the Lord will make His home with them, John 14:23; they have faith in God,[2] Mark 11:22; their works have been performed from God, John 3:21. All this is summed up in the words,

As many as received Him, to them He gave power to be children of God, to those believing in His name, who were born, not of blood, nor of the will of the flesh, nor of the will of man, but of God. John 1:12,13.

To believe in the name of the Son of God means to believe the Word and lead a life in keeping with it. The will of the flesh stands for the self, which is basically evil, occupying the human will, and the will of man for the self, which is basically falsity arising from evil, occupying the human understanding. People are born of the will of the flesh and the will of man when their will and actions, and their thought and utterances, spring from the self, but they are born of God when these spring from the Lord. In short, what is good does not come from people; what is good comes from the Lord.

---

1. A literal representation of the original Greek, which is taken to mean *wedding guests*
2. The Latin here may be rendered *they have the faith of God*, but the verb in the original Greek expresses a direct command or exhortation to have the faith of God or to have faith in God

Quod quantum homo fugit mala ut peccata, tantum faciat bona non a se sed a Domino

18   Quis non scit et scire potest quod mala impediant quin Dominus ad hominem intrare possit? Malum enim est infernum, et Dominus est caelum, ac infernum et caelum opposita sunt. Quantum itaque homo est in uno, tantum non potest esse in altero, unum enim agit contra alterum, et destruit.

19   Homo, quamdiu est in mundo, in medio est inter infernum et caelum – infra est infernum et supra est caelum – et tunc tenetur in libero convertendi se aut ad infernum aut ad caelum. Si se convertit ad infernum, avertit se a caelo; si autem convertit se ad caelum, avertit se ab inferno. Seu quod idem est: homo, quamdiu est in mundo, in medio stat inter Dominum et diabolum, ac tenetur in libero convertendi se aut ad unum aut ad alterum. Si se convertit ad diabolum, se avertit a Domino; si autem convertit se ad Dominum, avertit se a diabolo. Seu quod idem est: homo, quamdiu in mundo est, in medio est inter malum et bonum, et tenetur in libero convertendi se aut ad unum aut ad alterum. Si se convertit ad malum, avertit se a bono; si autem convertit se ad bonum, avertit se a malo.

20   Dicitur quod homo teneatur in libero convertendi se huc illuc. Hoc liberum est cuivis homini non ab ipso sed a Domino, quare dicitur quod teneatur in illo. De aequilibrio inter caelum et infernum, et quod homo sit in illo, et inde in libero, videatur in opere **De Caelo et Inferno**, n.589-596 et n.597-603. Quod quivis homo in libero teneatur, et quod id nemini auferatur, videbitur in suo loco.

21   Ex his manifeste patet quod quantum homo fugit mala, tantum apud Dominum et in Domino sit; et quantum in Domino est, tantum faciat bona non a se sed a Domino.

To the extent that people shun as sins the things that are evil they do those that are good not from self but from the Lord

18   Is there anyone who does not know or is incapable of knowing that evil things prevent the Lord's coming into a person? For evil constitutes hell, and the Lord constitutes heaven, and hell and heaven are opposites. Therefore to the extent people are in one they cannot be in the other, for one acts against and is destructive of the other.

19   As long as people are in this world they are living midway between hell and heaven, with hell below and heaven above, and during this time they are maintained in freedom to turn themselves either in the direction of hell or in that of heaven. If they turn to face hell they turn away from heaven, but if they turn to face heaven they turn away from hell. Or what amounts to the same thing, as long as people are in the world they stand midway between the Lord and the devil, and are maintained in freedom to turn themselves to face either one or the other. If they turn to face the devil they turn away from the Lord, but if they turn to face the Lord they turn away from the devil. Or what also amounts to the same thing, as long as people are in the world they are midway between evil and good, and are maintained in freedom to turn themselves to face either one or the other. If they turn to face evil they turn away from good, but if they turn to face good they turn away from evil.

20   As has just been said, people are maintained in freedom to turn themselves in this direction or in that. This freedom people have does not originate in themselves but comes from the Lord, and this is the reason for saying that they are maintained in it. Regarding the equilibrium between heaven and hell, and the fact that people are maintained in a state of equilibrium, and therefore in freedom, see the work **Heaven and Hell**, §§589-596 and §§597-603. The fact that people are maintained in this freedom and none can take it away from them will be seen in the proper place to present it.

21   From all this it is plainly evident that to the extent people flee from things that are evil they abide with and in the Lord; and to the extent they abide in the Lord they do things that are good not

Inde haec communis lex resultat – **Quod quantum quis fugit mala, tantum faciat bona**.

22 Sed duo requisita sunt: unum, quod homo fugere debeat mala quia peccata sunt, hoc est, quia sunt infernalia et diabolica, ita contra Dominum et contra leges Divinas; alterum, quod homo debeat fugere mala ut peccata sicut ab seipso, sed sciat et credat quod a Domino. Sed de hoc et de illo requisito dicetur in articulis subsequentibus.

23 Ex his sunt tria haec consequentia –

i Quod si homo bona vult et facit, antequam fugit mala ut peccata, bona non sint bona

ii Quod si homo pia cogitat et loquitur, et non fugit mala ut peccata, pia non sint pia

iii Quod si homo scit et sapit multa, et non fugit mala ut peccata, usque non sapiat

24 i **Quod si homo bona vult et facit, antequam fugit mala ut peccata, bona non sint bona**, est quia non prius est in Domino, ut supra dictum est. Prout, si det pauperibus, opem ferat egenis, impendat templis et hospitalitiis, benefaciat ecclesiae, patriae, et concivibus, doceat Evangelium et convertat, agat justitiam in judiciis, sinceritatem in negotiis, et rectitudinem in operis, et tamen mala ut peccata nihili facit – sicut fraudes, adulteria, odia, blasphemias, et similia alia – tunc non aliter potest facere bona quam quae intus mala sunt. Facit enim illa ex se et non ex Domino, ita est ipse in illis et non Dominus; et bona in quibus ipse homo est sunt omnia conspurcata malis ejus, et spectant ipsum et mundum. Attamen eadem illa facta quae supra recensita sunt, interius bona sunt si homo fugit mala ut peccata – prout fraudes, adulteria, odia, blasphemias, et similia alia – facit enim illa a Domino, et vocantur **in Deo facta**, Joh.3:19-21.

from self but from the Lord. Springing as a result from this is the following general rule – **To the extent that anyone shuns things that are evil that person does those that are good.**

22   But two things are required. One is that people should shun evil things because they are forms of sin, that is, because they belong to hell and the devil, and so are contrary to the Lord and Divine laws; the other is that people should shun evil ways as forms of sin as though they do so by themselves, but should realize and believe it is by the Lord that they do so. But this and the previous requirement will be discussed in subsequent sections.

23   Following on from all this there are these three matters to be considered –

i   If people intend and perform good deeds before they shun as sins those which are evil, their good deeds are not good

ii   If people think and utter holy thoughts but do not shun evil deeds as sins, their holy thoughts and utterances are not holy

iii   Though they may possess much knowledge and wisdom, nonetheless people are not wise if they do not shun evil deeds as sins

24   i **If people intend and perform good deeds before they shun as sins those which are evil, their good deeds are not good**. This is because they do not, as mentioned above, first abide in the Lord. If for instance they give to the poor, help the needy, endow places of worship and those which provide care, do things that benefit church, country, and fellow citizens, teach the Gospel and help to convert people, act justly when giving judgments, honestly when making business deals, and uprightly when turning out pieces of work, and yet totally disregard evil actions as sins – such as those involving fraud, adultery, hatred, blasphemy, and others like these – they cannot perform any good deeds other than those which are inwardly bad. For they perform them from self, not the Lord, and so it is they themselves that are at the centre of those deeds, not the Lord, and good deeds which have the doers themselves within them are polluted every one with the doers' evil ways, and have self and the world in view. But the same good deeds which have been listed above are inwardly good if people shun evil actions as sins – for instance, those involving fraud, adultery, hatred, blasphemy, and other actions such as these – because the things they do spring from the Lord, and are called **deeds carried out in God**, John 3:19-21.

25 ii **Quod si homo pia cogitat et loquitur, et non fugit mala ut peccata, pia non sint pia**, est quia non est in Domino. Ut, si frequentat templa, devote auscultat praedicationes, legit Verbum et pietatis libros, obit Sacramentum Caenae, quotidie fundit preces, imo si multum cogitat de Deo et de salute, et tamen mala quae sunt peccata, nihili facit – ut fraudes, adulteria, odia, blasphemias, et similia alia – tunc non potest aliter cogitare et loqui pia quam quae intus non pia sunt, nam ipse homo cum malis suis est in illis. Haec quidem tunc nescit, sed tamen inibi sunt et coram illo latent; est enim sicut fons, cujus aqua est impura ex vena. Exercitia pietatis ejus vel sunt modo solennia ex habitu, vel sunt meritoria, vel sunt hypocritica. Ascendunt quidem versus caelum, sed reflectunt se in via et decidunt, sicut fumi in aere.

26 Datum est videre et audire multos post mortem qui enumeraverunt bona sua opera et pietatis exercitia, quae nunc supra, n.24,25, memorata sunt, et plura adhuc. Inter illos etiam vidi quosdam habere lampades et non oleum. At inquisitum est num fugerint mala ut peccata, ac inventi quod non, quare illis dictum est quod mali sint. Visi etiam postea intrare cavernas ubi similes mali erant.

27 iii **Quod si homo scit et sapit multa, et non fugit mala ut peccata, usque non sapiat**, est ex simili causa de qua prius, quod sapiat a se et non a Domino. Prout, si sciat doctrinam ecclesiae suae, et omnia ejus ad amussim; si sciat confirmare illa per Verbum et per ratiocinia; si sciat doctrinas omnium ecclesiarum a saeculis, et simul edicta omnium conciliorum; imo si sciat veritates, et quoque videat et intelligat illas; ut si sciat quid fides, quid charitas, quid pietas, quid paenitentia et remissio peccatorum, quid regeneratio, quid Baptismum et Sacra Caena, quid Dominus, et quid redemptio et salvatio – is usque non sapit si non fugit mala ut peccata. Sunt enim cognitiones absque vita, quia modo intellectus ejus et non

25 ii **If people think and utter holy thoughts but do not shun evil deeds as sins, their thoughts and utterances are not holy.** This is because such people do not abide in the Lord. They may go to places of worship frequently, listen to sermons reverently, read the Word and religious books, attend the Holy Supper, and every day pour forth prayers. They may indeed give much thought to God and to salvation, but if they make light of evil ways that are sins – such as those involving them in fraud, adultery, hatred, blasphemy, and the like – they cannot do other than think and utter holy thoughts which inwardly are not holy. For those people themselves along with their evil ways reside within what they are thinking and saying. They are not, it is true, aware of this at the time, but such people themselves and their evil ways nevertheless reside there, hidden from their sight. For these people are like a spring whose water is impure right from source. Their religious observances are either no more than habitual performances of ritual, or they are carried out to gain merit, or they are hypocritical. Those observances indeed rise upwards to heaven, but as they do so they turn about and sink down, like plumes of smoke up in the air.

26 I have been allowed to see and listen to many after death who listed their good works and performance of religious observances mentioned just above in §§24,25, and more besides. Among those people I have also seen some or other of them who had lamps but no oil. When inquiries were made as to whether they had shunned evil deeds as sins they were found not to have done so, and were therefore told they were evil. I also saw them after that enter caverns where similarly evil ones were.

27 iii **Though they may possess much knowledge and wisdom, nonetheless people are not wise if they do not shun evil deeds as sins.** This is so for a reason similar to the one given before – that their wisdom springs from self, not from the Lord. They may, for instance, be acquainted with the teaching of their church, with a proper knowledge of all aspects of it; they may be able to substantiate all they know by means of the Word and the use of reasonings; they may be acquainted with the teachings of all the churches down the centuries, and at the same time with the decisions of all the councils. Indeed they may have a knowledge of truths, also perceive them and understand them; they may, for instance, know all about faith, the love of others, holiness, repentance and forgiveness of sins, regeneration, Baptism and the Holy Supper, the Lord, redemption and salvation. Even so, they are not wise if they do not shun evil deeds as sins. That knowledge they possess is devoid of life, because it is solely part of their understanding and not at the same time of their

simul voluntatis ejus sunt; et quae talia sunt, tempore pereunt, ex causa de qua supra, n.15. Post mortem etiam ipse homo ejicit illa, quia cum amore voluntatis ejus non concordant. Sed usque cognitiones maxime necessariae sunt, quia illae docent quomodo homo faciet; et cum facit illas, tunc apud illum vivunt. Non prius.

28   Haec omnia quae hactenus dicta sunt, Verbum multis in locis docet, ex quibus sequentia modo adducentur. Verbum docet quod nemo possit in bono esse et simul in malo seu, quod idem, quod nemo possit quoad animam in caelo esse et simul in inferno. Docet hoc in his –

Nemo potest duobus dominis servire, nam aut unum odio habebit et alterum amabit, aut uni adhaerebit et alterum contemnet. Non potestis Deo servire et mammonae. Matt.6:24.

Quomodo potestis bona loqui, cum mali estis? Ex abundantia cordis os loquitur. Bonus homo ex bono thesauro cordis sui emittit bona, et malus homo ex malo thesauro emittit mala. Matt.12:34,35.

Arbor bona non facit fructum malum, neque arbor mala facit fructum bonum. Omnis arbor ex proprio fructu cognoscitur; non enim ex spinis colligunt ficus, neque ex rubo vindemiant uvam. Luc.6:43,44.

29   Verbum docet quod nemo possit bonum facere a se sed a Domino. Dixit Jesus,

Ego sum vitis, et Pater Meus vinitor. Omnem palmitem in Me non ferentem fructum, tollit illum; omnem autem fructum ferentem, putabit illum, ut plus fructus ferat. Manete in Me, etiam Ego in vobis; quemadmodum palmes non potest ferre fructum a se ipso, nisi manserit in vite, ita neque vos, nisi in Me manseritis. Ego sum vitis, vos palmites. Qui manet in Me, et Ego in illo, hic fert fructum multum, quia sine Me non potestis facere quicquam. Nisi quis manserit in Me, ejectus est foras sicut palmes, et arefactus est et colligunt illum, et in ignem conjiciunt, et comburitur. Joh.15:1-6.

30   Verbum docet quod quantum homo non purificatus est a malis, bona ejus non sint bona, nec pia ejus sint pia, nec sapiat, et vicissim, in his –

will or intent; and being like this it perishes in the course of time, for the reason stated above in §15. What is more, those people after death cast that knowledge aside, because it does not accord with the love in their will or intent. Nevertheless acquisition of that knowledge is absolutely necessary, because it teaches people how they are to act; and when they act in accordance with it, it has life in them. Not before.

28   All this that has been mentioned so far is the teaching contained in many places in the Word, of which just the following ones will be quoted here. The teaching of the Word is that no one can be governed by good and at the same time by evil or, what amounts to the same thing, no one's soul can be in heaven and at the same time in hell. That is the teaching in these places –

None can serve two lords, for either they will hate the one and love the other, or they will cling to the one and despise the other. You cannot serve God and mammon. Matt.6:24.
How can you speak good things when you are evil? Out of the abundance of the heart the mouth speaks. Good people out of the good treasure of their heart send out good things, and evil people out of the evil treasure send out evil things. Matt.12:34,35.
A good tree does not bear bad fruit, nor does a bad tree bear good fruit. Every tree is known by its own fruit; for people do not collect figs from thorns, nor do they gather grapes from a bramble bush. Luke 6:43,44.

29   The teaching of the Word is that none can from themselves do what is good, only from the Lord. Jesus said –

I am the vine, and My Father is the vine dresser. Every branch in Me that does not bear fruit He takes away, but every one that does bear fruit He prunes, that it may bear more fruit. Abide in Me, and I in you; as the branch cannot bear fruit by itself unless it abides in the vine, neither can you unless you abide in Me, I am the vine, you are the branches. Those who abide in Me, and I in them, they it is who bear much fruit, for apart from Me you cannot do anything. If any do not abide in Me they are cast out as a branch and become withered, and people gather them and throw them into the fire, and they are burned. John 15:1-6.

30   The teaching of the Word is that to the extent people have not been cleansed from evil things their good deeds are not good, neither are their holy thoughts holy, nor are they wise, and to the extent they have been cleansed the reverse is so. This teaching is expressed in these words –

Vae vobis, Scribae et Pharisaei, hypocritae, quia similes vos facitis sepulchris dealbatis, quae foris quidem apparent pulchra, intus vero plena sunt ossibus mortuorum et omni immunditie. Sic etiam vos foris quidem apparetis justi, intus vero pleni estis hypocrisi et iniquitate. Vae vobis, quia purgatis exterius poculi et patinae, interiora vero plena sunt rapina et intemperantia. Pharisaee caece, purga prius interius poculi et patinae, ut fiat etiam exterius mundum. Matt.23:25-28.

Tum ex his apud Esaiam,

Audite verbum Jehovae, principes Sodomae; audite legem Dei nostri, popule Gomorrhae. Quid Mihi multitudo sacrificiorum vestrorum? Ne addite adducere mincham vanitatis; suffitus abominatio Mihi est. Novilunium et sabbathum – non possum ferre iniquitatem. Novilunia et festa stata vestra odit anima Mea. Unde quando expanditis manus vestras, occulto oculos Meos a vobis; etiam si multiplicatis orationem, non Ego audiens; manus vestrae sanguinibus plenae sunt. Lavate vos, purificate vos, removete malitiam operum vestrorum a coram oculis Meis, cessate malum facere. Si fuerint peccata vestra sicut coccinea, sicut nix albescent; si rubra fuerint, sicut lana erunt. 1:10-18.

Haec in summa sunt, quod nisi homo fugit mala, omnia cultus ejus non bona sint, similiter omnia ejus opera, nam dicitur, Non possum ferre iniquitatem, purificate vos, removete malitiam operum vestrorum, cessate malum facere. Apud Jeremiam,

Revertimini quisque a via sua mala, et bona reddite opera vestra. 35:15.

Quod iidem nec sapient, apud Esaiam,

Vae sapientibus in oculis suis, et coram faciebus suis intelligentibus. 5:21.

Apud eundem,

Peribit sapientia sapientium, ac intelligentia intelligentium. Vae illis qui profunde sapiunt, et fiunt in tenebris opera illorum. 29:14,15.

Woe to you, Scribes and Pharisees, hypocrites, for you make yourselves like whitewashed sepulchres, which outwardly do indeed appear beautiful, but within are full of dead people's bones and all uncleanness. So too do you outwardly appear righteous, but inwardly you are full of hypocrisy and iniquity. Woe to you, for you cleanse the outside of the cup and the plate, but the inner parts are full of extortion and lack of restraint. Blind Pharisee, cleanse first the inside of the cup and the plate, so that the outside also may be made clean. Matt.23:25-28.[1]

The same teaching is presented by the following declarations in Isaiah,

Hear the word of Jehovah, you rulers of Sodom; hear the law of our God, you people of Gomorrah. What to Me is the multitude of your sacrifices? Bring no more a vain meal-offering; incense is an abomination to Me. New moon and sabbath – I cannot bear iniquity. Your new moons and appointed feasts My soul hates. Therefore when you spread out your hands I will surely hide My eyes from you; even if you offer much prayer I am not listening; your hands are full of blood. Wash yourselves, make yourselves clean, remove the wickedness of your doings from before My eyes; cease to do evil. Though your sins are like scarlet, they will be as white as snow; though they are red they will be like wool. 1:10-18.

The teaching of these declarations is in short that unless people shun evil deeds none of their worship is good, nor similarly any of their doings, for it says, I cannot bear iniquity, make yourselves clean, remove the wickedness of your doings, cease to do evil. In Jeremiah,

Turn back each of you from your evil way, and cause your works to be good. 35:15.

The fact that such people are not wise, either, is the teaching in Isaiah, 2

Woe to those who are wise in their own eyes, and in their own sight are intelligent. 5:21.

In the same prophet,

The wisdom of the wise ones will perish, and the intelligence of the intelligent. Woe to those who are profoundly wise, and their works are performed in the dark. 29:14,15.

---

1   The first 'Woe…' quoted here stands in the Gospel after the second

Et alibi apud eundem,

Vae descendentibus in Aegyptum pro auxilio, et super equis innituntur, et confidunt super curru, quod multus, et super equitibus, quod validi sint, sed non respiciunt ad Sanctum Israelis, et Jehovam non quaerunt. Sed surget contra domum malignorum, et contra auxilium operantium iniquitatem. Nam Aegyptus homo et non Deus, et equi ejus caro et non spiritus. 31:1-3.

Ita describitur propria intelligentia. Aegyptus est scientia, equus est intellectus inde; currus est doctrina inde, eques est intelligentia inde, de quibus dicitur, Vae illis qui non respiciunt ad Sanctum Israelis, et Jehovam non quaerunt. Destructio eorum per mala intelligitur per Surget contra domum malignorum, et contra auxilium operantium iniquitatem. Quod illa sint ex proprio, et ideo non in illis vita, intelligitur per quod Aegyptus homo et non Deus, et quod equi ejus caro et non spiritus. Homo et caro sunt proprium hominis, Deus et spiritus sunt vita a Domino, equi Aegypti sunt propria intelligentia. Talia sunt plura in Verbo de intelligentia a se et de intelligentia a Domino, quae modo per sensum spiritualem patent.
    Quod nemo salvetur per bona a se, quia non sunt bona, patet ex his –

Non omnis dicens Mihi, Domine, Domine, intrabit in regnum caelorum, sed faciens voluntatem Patris Mei. Multi dicent Mihi in die illo, Domine, Domine, nonne per nomen Tuum prophetavimus, et per nomen Tuum daemonia ejecimus, et in nomine Tuo multas virtutes fecimus? Sed tunc confitebor illis, Non novi vos, discedite a Me, **operantes iniquitatem**. Matt.7:21-23.

Et alibi,

Tunc incipietis foris stare, et pulsare januam, dicentes, Domine, aperi nobis; et incipietis dicere, Edimus coram Te, et bibimus, et in plateis nostris docuisti. Sed dicet, Dico vobis, non novi vos unde sitis, discedite a Me, omnes **operarii iniquitatis**. Luc.13:25-27.

---

6   *om* homo et *VI*
7   caro et non: caro non *VI*

And in another place in the same prophet,

Woe to those who go down into Egypt for help, and rely on horses and trust in chariots because they are many, and on horsemen because they are extremely strong, but do not look to the Holy One of Israel and do not seek Jehovah. But He will arise against the house of evildoers and against the help of those working iniquity. For Egypt is man and not God, and its horses are flesh and not spirit. 31:1-3.

This is a description of self-intelligence. Egypt means knowledge, horse means the understanding derived from this, chariot means teaching derived from it, and horseman means intelligence derived from it. Referring to all these it says, Woe to those who do not look to the Holy One of Israel and do not seek Jehovah. The destruction of them through evil deeds is meant by, He will arise against the house of evildoers and against the help of those working iniquity. Their origin in self, and consequently having no life in them, is meant by Egypt being man and not God, and its horses being flesh and not spirit. Man and flesh mean the human self, God and spirit mean life from the Lord, and horses of Egypt mean self-intelligence. There are many places such as these in the Word that refer to intelligence derived from self and intelligence derived from the Lord, which only the spiritual sense makes clear.

    The teaching that no one is saved through good deeds which have their origin in self because these are not good is evident from the following – 3

Not all who say to Me, Lord, Lord, will enter the kingdom of heaven but those who do the will of My Father. Many will say to Me on that day, Lord, Lord, did we not prophesy by Your name, and by Your name cast out demons, and in Your name do many mighty works? But then I will confess to them, I do not know you; depart from Me, **you workers of iniquity**. Matt.7:21-3.

And in another place,

Then you will begin to stand outside and knock at the door, saying, Lord, open for us; and you will begin to say, We ate in Your presence, and drank, and You taught in our streets. But He will say, I tell you, I do not know where you are from; depart from Me, all **you workers of iniquity**. Luke 13:25-7.

Similes enim sunt Pharisaeo qui in Templo stans orabat, dicens quod non esset sicut reliqui homines, rapax, injustus, maechus, quod jejunaret bis in septimana, et daret decimas omnium quae possidebat, Luc.18:11-14; sunt etiam illi qui vocantur inutiles servi, Luc.17:10.

31   Veritas est quod nullus homo possit facere bonum a se, quod bonum est. Sed per id destruere omne bonum charitatis – quod homo qui fugit mala ut peccata facit – est enorme, est enim e diametro contra Verbum, quod mandat quod homo faciet. Est contra praecepta amoris in Deum et amoris erga proximum, a quibus mandatis Lex et Prophetae pendent; et est sugillare et supplantare omne religionis. Unusquisque enim scit quod religio sit bonum facere, et quod quisque secundum facta judicetur. Omnis homo talis est ut possit fugere mala sicut a se ipso ex potentia Domini, si illam imploret; et quod postea facit, est bonum a Domino.

For these people are like the Pharisee who, standing and praying in the Temple, said that he was not like everyone else – an extortioner, unjust, an adulterer – that he fasted twice in a week, and gave tithes of all that he possessed, Luke 18:11-14. They are also those who are called unprofitable servants, Luke 17:10.

31   Though it is true that none are able from self to do anything good which is truly good, the use of this truth to invalidate every good deed of love of others performed by those who shun evil deeds as sins is monstrous. To do this is to go completely against the Word, which commands people to do what is good. It goes against the commands to love God and love your neighbour, on which depend the Law and the Prophets; it makes a mockery of and does away with the whole of religion. For everyone knows that religion consists in doing what is good and that all are judged according to their deeds. All are able – in the Lord's strength, if they beg for it – to shun evil ways, as if they are doing so from themselves; and what they do afterwards is good that springs from the Lord.

Quod quantum quis fugit mala ut peccata, tantum amet vera

32   Sunt duo universalia quae procedunt a Domino, Divinum Bonum et Divinum Verum; Divinum Bonum est Divini Amoris Ipsius et Divinum Verum est Divinae Sapientiae Ipsius. Illa duo in Domino unum sunt, et inde ut unum procedunt ab Ipso, sed non ut unum recipiuntur ab angelis in caelis et ab hominibus in terris. Sunt angeli et homines qui plus ex Divino Vero recipiunt quam ex Divino Bono, et sunt qui plus ex Divino Bono quam ex Divino Vero. Inde est quod caeli in duo regna distinguantur, quorum unum vocatur regnum caeleste, alterum regnum spirituale. Caeli qui plus ex Divino Bono recipiunt, constituunt regnum caeleste, qui autem plus ex Divino Vero, constituunt regnum spirituale. De binis his regnis, in quae caeli distincti sunt, videatur in opere **De Caelo et Inferno**, n.20-28.

Sed usque angeli omnium caelorum tantum in sapientia et intelligentia sunt, quantum bonum apud illos unum facit cum vero; bonum quod non unum facit cum vero, hoc illis non est bonum, vicissim etiam verum quod non unum facit cum bono, hoc illis non est verum. Inde patet quod bonum conjunctum vero faciat amorem et sapientiam apud angelum et apud hominem; et quia angelus est angelus ex amore et sapientia apud illum, similiter homo, patet quod bonum conjunctum vero faciat ut angelus sit angelus caeli, et quod homo sit homo ecclesiae.

33   Quoniam Bonum et Verum unum sunt in Domino ac ut unum procedunt ab Ipso, sequitur quod bonum amet verum, et verum amet bonum, ac velint unum esse. Similiter oppositum illorum; quod malum amet falsum, et falsum malum, ac velint unum esse. Conjunctio boni et veri in sequentibus vocabitur conjugium caeleste, et conjunctio mali et falsi conjugium infernale.

To the extent that people shun evil deeds as sins, they love truths

32   There are two universal realities which emanate from the Lord, Divine Goodness and Divine Truth. Divine Goodness is an emanation of His Divine Love, and Divine Truth is an emanation of His Divine Wisdom. Within the Lord these two exist as one, and therefore emanate from Him as one, but they are not received as one by angels in heaven and by people on earth. There are angels and people who are more receptive of Divine Truth than they are of Divine Goodness, and there are those more receptive of Divine Goodness than of Divine Truth. This explains why the heavens are divided into two kingdoms, one being called the celestial kingdom, the other the spiritual kingdom. Heavens more receptive of Divine Goodness compose the celestial kingdom, whereas those more receptive of Divine Truth compose the spiritual kingdom. For more about these two kingdoms that the heavens are divided into, see the work **Heaven and Hell**, §§20-28.

Nevertheless angels in all of the heavens are in possession of wisdom and intelligence, to the extent that the goodness with them makes one with truth. If the goodness does not make one with the truth it is not goodness they possess; and conversely, if the truth does not make one with the goodness it is not truth they possess. From this it is evident that goodness linked to truth constitutes the love and wisdom an angel or a person possesses; and since angels are angels by virtue of the love and wisdom they possess, and the like is so in the case of people, it is evident that goodness linked to truth is what causes an angel to be an angel belonging to heaven, and it is what causes a person to be a person belonging to the church.

33   Since Goodness and Truth exist as one in the Lord and emanate from Him as one, it follows that goodness is in love with truth, and truth is in love with goodness, and the two desire to exist as one. Similarly so with the opposite of them; evil is in love with falsity, and falsity with evil, and the two desire to exist as one. From here on the combination of goodness and truth will be termed the heavenly marriage, and that of evil and falsity the hellish marriage.

34 Horum consequens est quod quantum quis fugit mala ut peccata, tantum amet vera, tantum enim in bono est, ut in mox praecedente articulo ostensum est. Tum vicissim, quod quantum quis non fugit mala ut peccata, tantum non amet vera, quia tantum non in bono est.

35 Potest quidem homo qui non fugit mala ut peccata, amare vera. Sed non amat illa quia vera sunt sed quia inserviunt famae, ex qua ei honor aut lucrum; quare si non inserviunt, non amat illa.

36 Bonum est voluntatis, verum est intellectus. Ab amore boni in voluntate procedit amor veri in intellectu, ab amore veri procedit perceptio veri, a perceptione veri cogitatio veri. Ex illis est agnitio veri, quae est fides in suo genuino sensu. Quod haec progressio ab amore boni ad fidem sit, demonstrabitur in transactione **De Divino Amore et Divina Sapientia**.

37 Quoniam bonum non est bonum nisi sit conjunctum vero, ut dictum est, consequenter bonum non prius existit; et tamen continue vult existere, quare ut existat, desiderat et comparat sibi vera. Ex his est nutritio ejus et formatio ejus. Haec causa est quod quantum quis in bono est, tantum amet vera, proinde quantum quis fugit mala ut peccata, nam tantum in bono est.

38 Quantum quis in bono est et ex bono amat vera, tantum amat Dominum, quoniam Dominus est ipsum Bonum et ipsum Verum. Est itaque Dominus apud hominem in bono et in vero; si hoc ex illo amatur, tunc Dominus amatur, et non aliter. Hoc Dominus docet apud Johannem,

Qui habet praecepta Mea et facit illa, ille est qui amat Me; qui vero non amat Me, verba Mea non servat. 14:21,24.

34   From all this it follows that to the extent people shun evil deeds as sins they love truths, for they are to that extent filled with goodness, as was shown in the section immediately before this. And conversely, to the extent people do not shun evil deeds as sins they do not love truths, because to that extent they are not filled with goodness.

35   It is possible, it is true, for people who do not shun evil deeds as sins to love truths. But such people are not in love with them because they are truths, but because those truths serve their personal renown, which brings them important positions or material gain. Therefore if truths do not serve them in that way they have no love of them.

36   Goodness belongs to the will or intent, truth to the understanding. From love of goodness in the will comes forth love of truth in the understanding, from love of truth comes forth perception of truth, and from perception of truth thought of truth. And from all these comes acceptance of truth, that is, faith in the true sense of the word. This progression from love of goodness to faith will be demonstrated in the book concerning **Divine Love and Wisdom**.[1]

37   Since goodness is not goodness if it does not exist linked to truth, as has been said, goodness consequently has no real existence before then. Yet there is a constant wanting to exist, and therefore so that it may come to exist it desires truths and gathers them to itself. These truths feed it and give shape to it. This being so, to the extent people are filled with goodness they love truths, and therefore to the extent people shun evil deeds as sins they love truths, because to that extent they are filled with goodness.

38   To the extent people are filled with goodness and moved by it to love truths they love the Lord, for the Lord is Goodness itself and Truth itself. The Lord is present with a person therefore within goodness and within truth; and if truth rooted in goodness is loved, then the Lord is loved, in this and no other way. This is the Lord's teaching in John,[2]

Those who have My commandments and do them, they are the ones who love Me; but those who do not love Me do not keep My words. 14:21,24.

  1   See – in the author's Preface to **Teaching of the New Jerusalem concerning the Lord** – the eighth of the nine subjects Swedenborg was intending to deal with in forthcoming publications
  2   In the following quotations of John's Gospel the two different Latin words *praecepta* and *mandata*, rendered *commandments* and *commands* here, translate the one Greek expression used in both places

Et alibi,

Si mandata Mea servaveritis, manebitis in amore Meo. Joh.15:10.

Praecepta, verba, et mandata Domini sunt vera.
39 Quod bonum amet verum, illustrari potest per comparationes cum sacerdote, milite, negotiatore, et artifice.
Cum **sacerdote**
Ille, si in bono sacerdotii est – quod est prospicere saluti animarum, docere viam ad caelum, ac ducere quos docet – is sicut est in illo bono, ita ex amore et ejus desiderio – comparat sibi vera quae doceat, et per quae ducat. Sacerdos autem qui non in bono sacerdotii est sed in jucundo functionis suae ex amore sui et mundi, quod solum illi bonum est, ille etiam ex amore et ejus desiderio comparat sibi illa in copia secundum jucundum, quod est ejus bonum, inspirans.
Cum **milite**
Si in amore militiae est, ac in tutela aut in fama sentit bonum, is ex bono hoc et secundum id comparat sibi scientiam ejus, et si praefectus est, intelligentiam ejus. Haec sunt sicut vera, ex quibus jucundum amoris, quod est bonum ejus, nutritur et formatur.
Cum **negotiatore**
Si se addixerat negotio ex amore ejus, is haurit cum voluptate omnia quae ut media illum amorem ingrediuntur et componunt. Haec quoque sunt sicut vera, cum negotiatio est bonum ejus.
Cum **artifice**
Si studio incumbit suae operae, et illam amat ut bonum suae vitae, is emit instrumenta, et per talia quae sunt scientiae ejus, perficit se; per haec facit opus suum ut sit bonum.
Ex his patet quod vera sint media per quae bonum amoris existit et fit aliquid, consequenter, quod bonum amet vera ut existat. Inde in Verbo per veritatem facere intelligitur facere ut bonum existat. Hoc intelligitur per Veritatem facere,

And in another place,

If you keep My commands you will remain in My love. John 15:10.

The Lord's commandments, words, and commands are the truths.

39   Light may be shed on the idea that goodness loves truth by the use of comparisons made with a priest, a soldier, a businessman, and a craftsman.

    Comparison with a **Priest**

If he has at heart the good performed by the priesthood – which consists in making provision for the salvation of souls, teaching the way to heaven, and guiding those he teaches – then, insofar as he does have that good at heart and so is acting from a love and desire for it, he acquires truths so that he may teach and guide a person by means of them. In the case of a priest however who does not have at heart the good performed by the priesthood, but from a love of self and the world takes pleasure in the office he holds – which for him is the only good – he too, from a love and desire for this good, acquires those truths in as great a measure as the pleasure, which for him is the only good, prompts him to do so.

    Comparison with a **Soldier**

If he has a love of soldiering, and sees his good to lie in defending his country or else in earning a reputation for himself, he is motivated and led by that good to acquire a knowledge or, if he is an officer, an understanding of this task. Such knowledge and understanding are like truths, which nourish and give shape to the pleasure that is a feature of his love and is his good.

    Comparison with a **Businessman**

If he has devoted himself to trading from a love of it he takes great pleasure in learning all the things which as means enter into and compose that love. These too are like truths, and trading is his good.

    Comparison with a **Craftsman**

If he applies himself conscientiously to the work he does, loving it as the good which is his in life, he buys tools and becomes better skilled by learning such things which make up the knowledge belonging to his craft. By means of tools and knowledge he causes his work to be his good.

    From these comparisons it is evident that truths are the means by which the good of love springs forth and presents itself within some outward form or other, consequently that good loves truths in order to spring forth. This is why in the Word the expression, To do the truth, is used to mean that good may spring forth. It is what is

Joh.3:21; Sermones Domini facere, Luc.6:47; Praecepta Ipsius facere, Joh.14:24; Verba Ipsius facere, Matt.7:24; Verbum Dei facere, Luc.8:21; ac Statuta et judicia facere, Lev.18:5. Hoc quoque est bonum et fructum facere, nam bonum et fructus est id quod existit.

40   Quod bonum amet verum et velit cum illo conjungi, illustrari etiam potest per comparationem cum cibo et aqua, seu cum pane et vino. Unum et alterum erit. Cibus aut panis solus non facit aliquid in corpore ad nutritionem, sed cum aqua aut vino; quare unum appetit et desiderat alterum. Per cibum et panem etiam in Verbo in sensu ejus spirituali intelligitur bonum, ac per aquam et vinum intelligitur verum.

41   Ex dictis nunc constare potest quod qui fugit mala ut peccata amet vera ac desideret illa; et quo plus fugit, eo plus amet et desideret, quia eo plus in bono est. Inde venit in conjugium caeleste, quod est conjugium boni et veri, in quo est caelum, et in quo erit ecclesia.

meant by Doing the truth, John 3:21; Doing the things the Lord says, Luke 6:47; Doing His commandments, John 14:24; Doing His words, Matt.7:24; Doing the Word of God, Luke 8:21; and Doing His statutes and judgments, Lev.18:5. The same is meant by doing good and bearing fruit, for good or fruit is that which comes forth.

40 Light may also be shed on the idea that good loves truth and wishes to be wedded to it by the use of a comparison made with food and water, or with bread and wine. One must go together with the other. Food or bread by itself does not in any way nourish the body; it does so only when accompanied by water or wine. The one therefore has an appetite and desire for the other. Furthermore in the Word, in its spiritual sense, good is meant by food and bread, and truth by water and wine.

41 From all that has just been stated it may be seen that people who shun evil deeds as sins love truths and desire them. And the more they shun those deeds, the more they come to love and desire the truths, because they are filled all the more with goodness. As a result of this they enter into the heavenly marriage, that is, the marriage of goodness and truth, in which heaven consists and the church ought to consist.

Quod quantum quis fugit mala ut peccata, tantum fidem habeat, et spiritualis sit

42 Fides et vita inter se distinctae sunt, sicut cogitare et facere; et quia cogitare est intellectus et facere est voluntatis, sequitur quod fides et vita inter se distinctae sint sicut intellectus et voluntas. Qui scit distinctionem harum, ille etiam scit distinctionem illorum, et qui scit conjunctionem harum, ille etiam scit conjunctionem illorum. Quare praemittendum est aliquid de intellectu et voluntate.

43 Sunt homini binae facultates, quarum una vocatur **Voluntas** et altera **Intellectus**. Illae inter se distinctae sunt, sed ita creatae ut unum sint, et cum unum sunt, vocantur **Mens**. Quare mens humana illae sunt, et omnis vita hominis ibi. Sicut omnia in universo quae secundum ordinem Divinum sunt se referunt ad bonum et verum, ita omnia apud hominem ad voluntatem et intellectum, nam bonum apud hominem est ejus voluntatis et verum apud illum est ejus intellectus. Sunt enim hae binae facultates receptacula et subjecta illorum; voluntas est receptaculum et subjectum omnium boni, ac intellectus est receptaculum et subjectum omnium veri. Bona et vera apud hominem non alibi sunt, ita non amor et fides sunt alibi, quoniam amor est boni et bonum est amoris, ac fides est veri et verum est fidei. Nihil magis interest scire quam quomodo voluntas et intellectus unam mentem faciunt. Faciunt unam mentem sicut bonum et verum faciunt unum, est enim simile conjugium inter voluntatem et intellectum, quale est inter bonum et verum. Quale hoc conjugium est, aliquantum in praecedente articulo dictum est; cui hoc addendum est, quod sicut bonum est ipsum esse rei, ac verum est existere rei inde, ita voluntas apud hominem est ipsum esse vitae

To the extent people shun evil deeds as sins they have faith and are spiritual

42   Faith and life are quite distinct from each other, as thinking and doing are; and because thinking belongs to the understanding and doing to the will, it follows that faith and life are quite distinct from each other, as understanding and will are. People who are aware of this distinctness between the latter two are also aware of that between the former; and people who are aware of the blending together of the latter two are also aware of the blending together of the former. For this reason something must be said first about understanding and will.

43   The human being has two faculties, one of which is called the **Will**, the other the **Understanding**. They are quite distinct from each other, yet have been created to exist as one; and when they do exist as one they are called the **Mind**. The human mind therefore consists of those two parts, and the whole of a person's life resides in them. Just as all things in the universe which are in accord with Divine order have reference to goodness and truth, so all things in the human being have reference to will and understanding, for the goodness present in people belongs to their will, and the truth present in them to their understanding. For these two faculties serve to receive and respond to them – the will to receive and respond to all forms of goodness, and the understanding to receive and respond to all forms of truth. They are the only place for forms of goodness and truth to be in the human being, and so are the only place for love and faith to be, since love pertains to goodness and goodness to love, while faith pertains to truth and truth to faith. There is nothing more important to know than how will and understanding constitute a single mind. They do so just as goodness and truth make one, for there is a marriage between will and understanding like that between goodness and truth. The nature of that marriage has been spoken of somewhat in the previous section, to which this needs to be added: just as goodness constitutes the inner being of something and truth the outward form it takes, so does the human will constitute the

2

ejus, ac intellectus existere vitae inde, nam bonum, quod est voluntatis, se in intellectu format, et certo modo se sistit videndum.

44. Quod homo possit multa scire, cogitare, et intelligere, et tamen non sapere, supra, n.27,28, ostensum est; et quia fidei est scire et cogitare, et magis adhuc intelligere, quod ita sit, ita potest homo credere quod fidem habeat, et tamen non habet. Causa quod non habeat, est quia in malo vitae est, ac malum vitae et verum fidei nusquam possunt unum agere. Malum vitae destruit verum fidei, quia malum vitae est voluntatis et verum fidei est intellectus, ac voluntas ducit intellectum ac facit ut unum secum agat; quare si aliquid in intellectu est quod non concordat cum voluntate, hoc quando homo sibi relictus est et ex suo malo et ejus amore cogitat, tunc verum, quod est in intellectu, vel ejicit vel cogit ut unum sit per falsificationem. Aliter apud illos qui in bono vitae sunt; hi sibi relicti ex bono cogitant, et verum, quod in intellectu est, amant, quia concordat. Ita fit conjunctio fidei et vitae, sicut est conjunctio veri et boni, atque haec et illa sicut est conjunctio intellectus et voluntatis.

45. Ex his nunc sequitur quod sicut homo fugit mala ut peccata, ita fidem habeat, quia ita in bono est, ut supra ostensum. Hoc confirmatur etiam ex suo contrario, quod qui non fugit mala ut peccata, non fidem habeat, quia in malo est, ac malum intrinsecus odit verum. Extrinsecus quidem potest ejus amicum agere, ac sufferre, imo amare ut in intellectu sit; at cum extrinsecum exuitur, quod fit post mortem, tunc verum suum amicum in mundo primum ejicit, postea negat quod verum sit, et demum aversatur.

46. Fides hominis mali est fides intellectualis, cui nihil boni ex voluntate inest. Ita est fides mortua, quae est sicut spiratio pulmonaris absque anima ejus ex corde; intellectus etiam correspondet pulmoni et voluntas cordi. Est quoque sicut pulchra meretrix, etiam ornata purpura et auro, quae

inner being of a person's life and the understanding the outward form that life takes, for goodness pertaining to the will gives form to itself in the understanding and in a certain kind of way manifests itself there.

44   It was shown above, in §§27-28, that people may come to know, think about, and have an understanding of many things, and yet be lacking in wisdom; and since faith consists in knowing and thinking, still more in understanding that something is true, people are therefore able to assume they possess faith, when in fact they do not. They do not possess it because evil is present in their life, and evil present in their life cannot ever act in unison with truth composing faith. The evil present in people's life destroys the truth that composes faith, because the evil inhabits the will or intent, the truth the understanding, and the will leads and forces the understanding to act in unison with it. Consequently if there is in the understanding any idea that does not accord with the will, then – when people are left to themselves, so that the evil present in them and their love of it govern what they think – they either expel truth grasped by the understanding or else falsify and compel the truth to act in unison. It is different in the case of those with goodness present in their life. Left to themselves they are governed in their thinking by goodness, and they love the truth present in their understanding because it accords with that goodness. Thus in the case of these people faith and life become linked together just as truth and goodness are linked together; and then truth and goodness go together, and faith and life together, just as understanding and will are linked together.

45   It follows then from all this that in the measure people shun evil deeds as sins they possess faith because they are in that measure filled with goodness, as shown above. The opposite also proves this to be so, in that people who do not shun evil deeds as sins do not possess faith, which is so because they are immersed in evil, and evil deep down hates truth. Superficially evil may indeed be friendly towards truth and suffer it, may even love its presence in the understanding, but when the superficial is stripped away, as happens after death, it first of all casts aside the truth it was friendly towards in the world, then denies it is the truth, and finally comes to loathe it.

46   The faith of an evil person is a faith which exists solely in the understanding and does not have in it any goodness supplied by the will. Thus it is a dead faith, which is like breathing, the function of the lungs, without the activation of it by the heart; and the understanding corresponds to the lungs and the will to the heart. It is also like a beautiful prostitute, adorned in purple and gold, who within is

interius maligna tabe scatet; meretrix etiam correspondet falsificationi veri, et inde in Verbo significat illam. Est etiam sicut arbor luxurians foliis et non dans fructus, quam hortulanus exscindit; etiam arbor significat hominem, folia et flores ejus vera fidei, et fructus bonum amoris. Alia vero est fides in intellectu, cui bonum ex voluntate inest. Haec fides est viva, et est sicut respiratio pulmonaris, cui anima est ex corde, et est sicut pulchra uxor amabilis viro ex castitate, et est sicut arbor fructifera.

47 Plura sunt quae apparent solius fidei esse, sicut quod Deus sit, quod Dominus, qui Deus, sit Redemptor et Salvator, quod caelum et infernum sint, quod vita post mortem sit, et plura alia, de quibus non dicitur quod facienda sed quod credenda. Haec fidei etiam mortua sunt apud hominem qui in malo est, sed viva apud hominem qui in bono est. Causa est quia homo qui in bono est non modo facit bene ex voluntate sed etiam cogitat bene ex intellectu, non solum coram mundo sed etiam coram se cum solus est. Aliter qui in malo est.

48 Dictum est quod illa appareant solius fidei esse, sed cogitatio intellectus trahit suum existere ex amore voluntatis, qui est esse cogitationis in intellectu, ut supra, n.43, dictum est. Quod enim quis ex amore vult, hoc vult facere, vult cogitare, vult intelligere, et vult loqui; seu, quod idem, quod quis ex voluntate amat, hoc amat facere, amat cogitare, amat intelligere, et amat loqui. Accedit, cum homo fugit malum ut peccatum, tunc ille in Domino est, ut supra ostensum, et Dominus operatur omnia. Quare Dominus, ad interrogantes Ipsum quid facerent ut operarentur opera Dei, dixit,

Hoc opus Dei est, ut credatis in Ipsum quem misit Ille. Joh.6:28,29.

Credere in Dominum non est modo cogitare quod Ipse sit sed etiam est facere verba Ipsius, ut alibi docet.

full of a dangerous disease; and a prostitute corresponds to the falsification of truth and therefore has this meaning in the Word. It is also like a tree full of leaves but producing no fruit, which the gardener cuts down; and a tree means a person, its leaves and blossom mean the truths of faith, and its fruit the goodness of love. But different from this is faith in the understanding which has within it goodness supplied by the will. This faith is alive; and it is like breathing lungs activated by the heart, like a beautiful wife who to her husband is lovable because of her chastity,[1] and like a tree that is fruitful.

47   There are many things which seem to be purely matters of faith, such as the existence of God; that the Lord, who is God, is Redeemer and Saviour; the existence of heaven and hell; life after death; and many more which are not spoken of as things to be done but things to be believed. These matters of faith are also dead in the case of people governed by what is evil, but alive in the case of those governed by what is good. The reason for this is that people governed by what is good are led not only by their will to do what is good but also by their understanding to think what is good; they do so not only when the world is looking but also when they are by themselves on their own. Different from all this are those governed by what is evil.

48   As I have said, those things seem to be purely matters of faith, but thought that takes place in the understanding derives its existence from love residing in the will, and this love is the inner being of the thought in the understanding, as stated above, in §43. For any who will something because they love it possess the will to do it, give thought to it, gain an understanding of it, and talk about it. Or, what amounts to the same thing, any who love something because they will it possess the love to do it, give thought to it, gain an understanding of it, and talk about it. Furthermore, when people shun evil as sin they abide in the Lord, as has been shown already, and the Lord accomplishes all things. This is why the Lord said to those asking Him what they had to do to accomplish the works of God,

This is the work of God, that you believe in Him whom He has sent. John 6:28,29.

Believing in the Lord involves not only thinking He exists but also doing His words, as is His teaching elsewhere.

---

1   The words *chaste* and *chastity* relate to the married as well as single state and therefore denote the pure and undefiled rather than the virginal and celibate

49   Quod qui in malis sunt non fidem habeant, utcunque putant se habere, ostensum est apud tales in mundo spirituali. Deducti sunt in societatem caelestem, unde spirituale fidei angelorum intravit in interiora fidei illorum qui eo deducti sunt, ex quo hi perceperunt quod illis modo naturale seu externum fidei esset, et non spirituale seu internum ejus. Quare ipsi confessi sunt quod prorsus nihil fidei haberent, et quod persuaserint sibi in mundo quod cogitare quod ita sit, ex omni causa, esset credere seu fidem habere. Sed aliter percepta est fides illorum qui non in malo fuerunt.

50   Ex his videri potest quid fides spiritualis et quid fides non spiritualis; quod fides spiritualis sit apud illos qui non peccata faciunt, nam qui non peccata faciunt, illi bona faciunt, non a se sed a Domino, videatur supra, n. 18-21, et per fidem fiunt spirituales. Fides apud illos est veritas. Hoc docet ita Dominus apud Johannem:

Hoc est judicium, quod lux venit in mundum, sed amaverunt homines magis tenebras quam lucem, erant enim opera illorum mala. Omnis qui mala facit odit lucem, et non venit ad lucem ne coarguantur opera ejus. Qui autem facit veritatem, venit ad lucem, ut manifestentur opera ejus, quoniam in Deo facta sunt. 3:19-21.

51   Haec quae hactenus dicta sunt confirmantur ex his in Verbo –

Bonus homo ex bono thesauro cordis sui profert bonum, at malus homo ex malo thesauro cordis sui profert malum, nam ex abundantia cordis loquitur os. Luc.6:45; Matt.12:35.

Per cor in Verbo intelligitur voluntas hominis; et quia homo inde cogitat et loquitur, dicitur, Ex abundantia cordis loquitur os.

Non quod intrat in os, immundum reddit hominem, sed quod egreditur ex corde, hoc immundum reddit hominem. Matt.15:11.

---

13   qui non peccata *VI*³: qui peccata *VI*¹, *VI*²

49 The fact that those immersed in evil ways do not possess real faith, no matter how much they may think they do, has been proved to me in the case of some people like them in the spiritual world. These were taken to a community in heaven, where the spiritual level of faith that the angels possessed stood in contrast to the inner side of the faith of these people taken there. As a result they could see that they possessed a merely natural or outward level of faith, not a spiritual or inward level of it. They therefore admitted that they did not possess any real faith at all, and that in the world they had convinced themselves that belief or possession of faith consisted in no more than thinking for whatever reason that a thing is so. But the faith of those not immersed in evil was seen to be quite different from that.

50 From all this it may be seen what the faith that is spiritual is and what the faith that is not spiritual is. Faith that is spiritual exists with those who commit no sins, for those who commit no sins perform good deeds, not from themselves but from the Lord, see §§18-21 above, and through that faith they become spiritual. The faith existing with them is the truth. The Lord teaches that this is so in John,

This is the judgment, that light has come into the world but people preferred darkness rather than light, because their deeds were evil. All who perform evil deeds hate the light and do not come to the light for fear that their deeds should be exposed. But those who do the truth come to the light, so that their deeds may be clearly seen, because they have been done in God. John 3:19-21.

51 What has been stated so far is borne out by the following in the Word –

Good people out of the good treasure of their heart bring forth good, and evil people out of the evil treasure of their heart bring forth evil, for out of the abundance of the heart the mouth speaks. Luke 6:45; Matt.12:35.

In the Word, heart is used to mean people's will or intent; and because people's thought and utterance springs from their will it is said, Out of the abundance of the heart the mouth speaks.

Not what enters the mouth renders a person unclean, but what comes out of the heart[1] renders the person unclean. Matt.15:11.

---

1 The Greek here, in Matt.15:11, means *out of the mouth*; but seven verses later the Lord says *what comes out of the mouth proceeds from the heart*

Per cor etiam hic intelligitur voluntas.

Jesus dixit de muliere quae unguento lavit pedes Ipsius, Remissa sunt ei peccata, quia multum amavit; et postea dixit, Fides tua te salvam fecit, Luc.7:46-50, ex quibus patet quod cum peccata remissa sunt, ita cum non sunt, fides salvet. Quod filii Dei et nati a Deo dicantur qui non in proprio voluntatis suae sunt, et inde non in proprio intellectus sui, hoc est, qui non in malo sunt et inde in falso, et quod illi sint qui credunt in Dominum, docet Ipse apud Johannem 1:12,13, qui locus explicatus videatur supra, n.17fin.

52   Conclusum ex his sequitur quod apud hominem non detur granum veri plus quam datur bonum, ita non granum fidei plus quam datur vita. Datur cogitatio quod ita sit, in intellectu, sed non agnitio quae fides, nisi detur consensus in voluntate. Ita fides et vita pari passu ambulant. Ex his nunc patet quod quantum quis fugit mala ut peccata, tantum fidem habeat et spiritualis sit.

---

4   fecit: facit *VI*

Here also heart is used to mean the will.

Jesus said – referring to the woman who anointed[1] His feet with ointment – Her sins are forgiven, for she loved much. And after this He said to her, Your faith has made you safe, Luke 7:46-50. From this it is evident that when sins have been forgiven, thus when they are no more, faith makes a person safe. Children of God and the Born of God are expressions describing those who are not governed by the self-seeking of their will and resulting self-intelligence of their understanding, that is, they are not governed by evil and resulting falsity; they are those who believe in the Lord, as is His teaching in John 1:12,13. See the end of §17 above for an explanation of this passage.

52 A conclusion following from all this is that not a grain more of truth than of goodness resides with a person, thus not a grain more of faith than of life does so. The thought that something is so may exist in the understanding, but not an acceptance of it which constitutes faith, unless assent exists in the will. So faith and life march in step with each other. From all this it is now evident that to the extent people shun evil deeds as sins, they have faith and are spiritual.

---

[1] literally *washed*

Quod Decalogus doceat quaenam mala sunt peccata

53 Quaenam gens in universo terrarum orbe non novit quod malum sit furari, adulterari, occidere, et false testari? Nisi haec scirent, et ne quis talia faciat, per leges caverent, actum foret de illis, nam societas, respublica, et regnum, absque illis legibus caderent. Quis autumare potest quod gens Israelitica prae omnibus aliis tam stupida fuerit ut ignoraverit quod illa essent mala? Quapropter mirari quis potest cur leges illae, universaliter in terrarum orbe cognitae, cum tanto miraculo e Monte Sinai ab Ipso Jehovah promulgatae fuerint. Sed audi: cum tali miraculo promulgatae fuerunt ut scirent quod leges illae non modo leges civiles et morales essent sed etiam leges spirituales, et quod facere contra illas non modo esset malum facere contra concivem et contra societatem sed etiam esset peccare contra Deum; quare leges illae, per promulgationem e Monte Sinai a Jehovah, factae sunt leges religionis; evidens enim est quod quicquid Jehovah Deus mandat, hoc mandet ut religionis sit, et quod faciendum propter Ipsum et propter hominem ut salvetur.

54 Illae leges quia fuerunt primitiae Verbi, et inde primitiae ecclesiae a Domino apud gentem Israeliticam instaurandae, et quia erant in brevi summario complexus omnium religionis, per quae conjunctio Domini cum homine et hominis cum Domino datur, ideo tam sanctae fuerunt ut nihil sanctius.

55 Quod sanctissimae fuerint, constare potest ex eo quod Ipse Jehovah, hoc est, Dominus, descenderit super Monte Sinai in igne et cum angelis, et illas viva voce inde promulgaverit, et quod populus per triduum se praeparaverit ad videndum et audiendum; quod mons circumseptus fuerit, ne quis

The Decalogue declares what the evil deeds are that are sins

53   What nation is there throughout the whole world that does not know that stealing, committing adultery, killing, or bearing false witness is evil? If nations did not know it, and by means of laws did not take steps to prevent anyone from doing those things, it would be all up with them, for community, state, and kingdom without those laws would fall apart. Does anyone imagine the Israelite nation to have been so stupid, more so than every other, that they did not know that such deeds were evil? Anyone may wonder therefore why those laws, known throughout the world, were proclaimed from Mount Sinai in such a miraculous fashion by Jehovah Himself. But listen to this: they were proclaimed in so miraculous a fashion in order that the people would come to know that those laws were not only civic and moral laws but also spiritual laws, and to know that to act contrary to them was not only to do harm to fellow citizen and to the community but also to sin against God. Those laws, through their proclamation from Mount Sinai by Jehovah, have consequently become religious laws; for it is plain that whatever Jehovah God commands He commands so that it may be a law of religion, and that it must be obeyed for His sake and for the sake of a person's salvation.

54   Because those laws were the first when the Word was given and they were therefore the first and most important ones of the church to be established by the Lord among the Israelite nation, and because they provided a short summary of the whole structure of their religion, through which the Lord was linked to a person and a person to the Lord, those laws were so holy that nothing could be more so.

55   Their supreme holiness becomes clear from the following details. Jehovah Himself, that is, the Lord, came down on Mount Sinai in fire and accompanied by angels, and proclaimed them from there in spoken words. For three days the people were getting themselves ready to watch and listen. A boundary was placed around the

accederet et moreretur; quod nec sacerdotes neque seniores appropinquarent sed Moses solus; quod Leges illae inscriptae fuerint binis tabulis lapideis digito Dei; quod Moses, cum illas secunda vice e monte deportavit, facie radiaverit; quod postea repositae fuerint in arca et haec in intimo tabernaculi, et super illam datum fuerit propitiatorium et super hoc positi cherubi ex auro; quod hoc fuerit sanctissimum ecclesiae illorum et vocatum sanctum sanctorum; quod extra velum, intra quod illud, collocata fuerint, quae repraesentaverunt sancta caeli et ecclesiae, quae erant candelabrum cum septem lucernis ex auro, altare suffimenti ex auro, et mensa super qua panes facierum obducta auro, cum aulaeis circumcirca ex bysso, purpura, et coccino. Sanctitas totius hujus tabernaculi non aliunde fuit quam ex Lege quae fuit in arca.

Propter sanctitatem tabernaculi ex Lege in arca, universus populus Israeliticus circum illud in ordine secundum tribus ex mandato castrametatus est, et in ordine post illud profectus est; et tunc supra illud fuit nubes interdiu et ignis noctu. Propter sanctitatem Legis illius, et praesentiam Domini in illa, loquebatur Dominus super propitiatorio inter cherubos cum Mose; et arca vocabatur Jehovah ibi. Tum non licuit Aharoni intrare intra velum, nisi cum sacrificiis et suffitu. Quia Lex illa erat ipsa sanctitas ecclesiae, ideo arca introducta fuit in Zionem a Davide, et postea in medio templi Hierosolymitani reposita, et faciebat ejus adytum.

Propter Domini praesentiam in Lege illa et circum illam, etiam miracula per arcam, in qua Lex illa fuit, facta sunt, ut, quod aquae Jordanis discissae sint, et quamdiu arca in medio quiescebat, populus in sicco transiverit; quod per circumlationem ejus muri Jerichuntis conciderint; quod Dagon deus Philisthaeorum coram illa decideret, et postea ad limen fani jaceret divulsus a capite; et quod propter illam percussi sint Bethschemitae ad plura millia; praeter alia. Haec omnia ex sola praesentia Domini in decem Ipsius verbis, quae sunt Praecepta Decalogi.

56 Tanta potentia et tanta sanctitas inerat isti Legi, etiam quia illa erat complexus omnium religionis, constabat enim ex binis tabulis, quarum una continet omnia quae a parte Dei sunt,

---

30 conciderint: ceciderint *VI*

mountain, to prevent anyone going near it and perishing. Neither priests nor elders were to approach it, only Moses. Those Laws were written, on two tablets of stone, with the finger of God. When Moses brought them down the second time his face was shining. After this they were put away in the ark, which resided in the inmost part of the tabernacle; on top of the ark existed the mercy seat, and on top of this were placed the cherubim of gold. This was the holiest part of their church and was called the holy of holies. Outside the veil which held the latter within it, objects were placed which represented holy aspects of heaven and the church. These were the lampstand with seven lamps made of gold; the altar of incense made of gold; and the table, overlaid with gold, on which the loaves of the presence were laid. And roundabout were curtains made of fine linen, purple, and scarlet. The holiness of the entire tabernacle was due solely to the presence of the Law within the ark.

2 On account of the holiness of the tabernacle, due to the presence of the Law within the ark, the whole people of Israel were commanded to pitch camp around it in order, according to their tribes, and after this to set off in order, when there was a cloud over it by day and fire by night. On account of the holiness of that Law and the Lord's presence within it the Lord spoke to Moses from above the mercy seat between the cherubim; indeed the ark was referred to as the place where Jehovah was. Also, Aaron was not permitted to go inside the veil other than with sacrifices and incense. Because the absolute holiness of the church lay within that Law the ark was brought by David to Zion, and at a later time it was placed in the middle of the temple in Jerusalem and constituted its innermost part.

3 On account of the Lord's presence within and around that Law, miracles too were accomplished by means of the ark in which the Law resided. There were, for instance, the miracles when the waters of the Jordan were split apart, and all the while the ark was resting in the middle, the people went across on dry ground; when the walls of Jericho collapsed as a result of its being carried round them; when Dagon the god of the Philistines fell to the ground in front of the ark, and after this lay over the threshold of the shrine severed from his head; when several thousand people of Bethshemesh were struck down because of it; besides many other miracles. All these things happened solely because of the Lord's presence in His ten words, that is, in the Commandments of the Decalogue.

56 Another reason why such great power and holiness existed within that Law was that it embraced the whole of religion, for it consisted of two tablets, one of which contains everything relating

et altera in complexu omnia quae a parte hominis sunt. Ideo Legis illius praecepta vocantur Decem Verba; ita vocantur quia decem significant omnia. Sed quomodo illa Lex est complexus omnium religionis, videbitur in sequente articulo.

57 Quoniam per Legem illam est conjunctio Domini cum homine et hominis cum Domino, vocatur illa Foedus et Testimonium – Foedus quia conjungit et Testimonium quia testator, nam foedus significat conjunctionem, ac testimonium testificationem ejus. Propterea tabulae illae erant binae, una pro Domino, altera pro homine. Conjunctio fit a Domino, sed tunc cum homo facit illa quae in ejus tabula scripta sunt. Dominus enim continue praesens est et operatur, et vult ingredi, sed homo ex suo libero, quod illi a Domino est, aperiet, nam dicit,

Ecce sto ad januam et pulso; si quis audiverit vocem Meam et aperuerit januam, ingrediar ad illum, et caenabo cum illo et ille Mecum. Apoc.3:20.

58 In altera tabula, quae est pro homine, non dicitur quod homo faciet hoc et illud bonum, sed dicitur quod non faciet hoc et illud malum, ut, Non occides, Non adulteraberis, Non furaberis, Non false testaberis, Non concupisces. Causa est quia homo non aliquod bonum potest facere a se, sed cum ille mala non facit, tunc bonum facit non a se sed a Domino. Quod homo possit fugere mala sicut a se ex potentia Domini, si illam imploret, videbitur in sequentibus.

59 Illa quae de Legis istius promulgatione, sanctitate, et potentia, supra, n.55, dicta sunt, inveniuntur in his locis in Verbo –

Quod Jehovah descenderit super Montem Sinai in igne, et quod tunc fumaverit et contremuerit mons; et quod fuerint tonitrua, fulgura, nubes gravis, et vox buccinae. Exod.19:16,18; Deut.4:11; 5:19-23.
Quod populus ante descensum Jehovae se praeparaverit et sanctificaverit per tres dies. Exod.19:10,11,15.
Quod mons circumseptus fuerit, ne quisquam ad ima ejus appropinquaret et accederet, ne moreretur; et quod nec sacerdotes sed Moses solus. Exod.19:12,13,20-23; 24:1,2.
Lex promulgata e Monte Sinai. Exod.20:2-14; Deut.5:6-18.

to God, and the second embraces everything relating to people. The commandments of that Law are consequently called The Ten Words; this they are called because ten stands for everything. How the Law embraces the whole of religion will be seen in the next section.

57   Since by means of that Law the Lord is linked to a person and a person to the Lord, it is called the Covenant and the Testimony – the Covenant because it serves to link them and the Testimony because it serves to bear witness to the link, for a covenant denotes a linking together and a testimony a witness to this. This is why there were the two tablets, one for the Lord, the other for persons. The linking together is accomplished by the Lord, but only when a person carries out what has been written on the tablet for persons. The Lord is constantly present and active, wishing to come in, but people must, in their freedom that the Lord imparts to them, open themselves up to Him, for He says,

Behold, I stand at the door and knock; if anyone hears My voice and opens the door I will come in to them and dine with them, and they with Me. Rev.3:20.

58   On the other tablet, which is for persons, it does not say that a person must perform this or that good deed but that a person must not perform this or that evil deed. It says, You shall not commit murder, You shall not commit adultery, You shall not steal, You shall not bear false witness, You shall not covet. The reason why is that people cannot do anything good from self, but when they do not perform evil deeds they then do what is good, not from self but from the Lord. The truth that people are able – by the Lord's power, if they earnestly seek it – to shun evil deeds as if from self will be seen in what follows.

59   The details mentioned above, in §55, concerning the proclamation, holiness, and power of that Law are found in the following places in the Word –

When Jehovah came down on Mount Sinai in fire the mountain was smoking and trembling, and there were thunders, lightnings, a thick cloud, and the sound of the trumpet. Exod.19:16,18; Deut.4:11; 5:22-26.

For three days before Jehovah came down the people were getting ready and consecrating themselves. Exod.19:10,11,15.

A boundary was placed round the mountain to prevent anyone approaching and coming near the foot of it, for fear that they would perish; not even the priests, only Moses, could do so. Exod.19:12,13,20-23; 24:1,2.

The Law was proclaimed from Mount Sinai. Exod.20:2-17; Deut.5:6-21.

DOCTRINA VITAE

Quod Lex illa inscripta sit binis tabulis lapideis digito Dei. Exod.31:18; 32:15,16: Deut.9:10.

Quod Moses, cum illas tabulas secunda vice e monte deportavit, facie radiaverit. Exod.34:29-35.

Quod tabulae repositae fuerint in arca. Exod.25:16; 40:20; Deut.10:5; 1 Reg.8:9.

Quod super arcam datum sit propitiatorium, et super hoc positi sint cherubi ex auro. Exod.25:17-21.

Quod arca, cum propitiatorio et cherubis, intimum tabernaculi fecerit; et quod candelabrum ex auro, altare suffimenti ex auro, et mensa super qua panis facierum obducta auro, exterius tabernaculi fecerint, ac decem aulaea ex bysso, purpura, et coccino, extimum ejus. Exod.25:1-fin.; 26:1-fin.; 40:17-28.

Quod locus ubi arca, vocatus sit Sanctum sanctorum. Exod.26:33.

Quod universus populus Israeliticus circum habitaculum in ordine secundum tribus castrametatus sit, et in ordine post illud profectus sit. Num.2:1-fin.

Quod tunc super habitaculo fuerit nubes interdiu et ignis noctu. Exod.40:38; Num.9:15,16-fin.; 14:14; Deut.1:33.

Quod Dominus loquutus sit cum Mose supra arcam inter cherubos. Exod.25:22; Num.7:89.

Quod arca, ex Lege in illa, dicta sit Jehovah ibi, dixit enim Moses cum arca proficiscebatur, Surge Jehovah, et cum quiescebat, Redi Jehovah. Num.10:35,36; et porro 2 Sam.6:2; Ps.132:7,8.

Quod propter sanctitatem istius Legis non licuerit Aharoni intrare intra velum, nisi cum sacrificiis et cum suffitu. Lev.16:2-14, seq.

Quod arca introducta sit in Zionem a Davide cum sacrificiis et cum jubilo. 2 Sam.6:1-19. Quod tunc Usa, quia tetegit illam, mortuus sit. Vers.6,7, ibi.

Quod arca in medio templi Hierosolymitani posita sit, ubi faciebat adytum. 1 Reg.6:19,seq.; 8:3-9.

Quod ex praesentia et potentia Domini in Lege quae in arca, aquae Jordanis discissae sint, et quamdiu illa in medio quiescebat, populus in sicco transiverit. Jos.3:1-17; 4:5-20.

Quod per circumlationem arcae muri Jerichuntis conciderint. Jos.6:1-20.

Quod Dagon, deus Philisthaeorum, coram arca in terram deciderit, et postea super limine fani jaceret divulsus a capite. 1 Sam.5:1-4.

Quod Bethschemitae propter arcam percussi sint ad plura millia. 1 Sam.6:19.

That Law was written, on two tablets of stone, with the finger of God. Exod.31:18; 32:15,16: Deut.9:10.

When Moses brought the tablets down a second time from the mountain his face was shining. Exod.34:29-35.

The tablets were put away in the ark. Exod.25:16; 40:20; Deut.10:5; 1 Kings 8:9.

On top of the ark existed the mercy seat, and on top of this were placed the cherubim of gold. Exod.25:17-21.

The ark, with mercy seat and cherubim, composed the inmost part of the tabernacle; the lampstand of gold, altar of burnt incense of gold, and table with loaves of the presence on it, overlaid with gold composed the outer part of the tabernacle; and the ten curtains of fine linen, purple, and scarlet the outermost part of it. Exod.25:1-end; 26:1-end; 40:17-28.

The place where the ark was, was called the holy of holies. Exod.26:33.

All the people of Israel pitched camp around the tabernacle in order, according to their tribes, and after this set off in order. Num.2:1-end.

At this time there was a cloud over the tabernacle by day, and fire by night. Exod.40:38; Num.9:15,16-end; 14:14; Deut.1:33.

The Lord spoke to Moses from above the ark between the cherubim. Exod.25:22; Num.7:89.

Because of the Law within it the ark was referred to as the place where Jehovah was, for when the ark set out Moses said, Arise, O Jehovah; and when it rested, Return, O Jehovah.

Num.10:35,36; and in addition, 2 Sam.6:2; Ps.132:7,8.

On account of the holiness of that Law Aaron was not permitted to go inside the veil other than with sacrifices and incense.

Lev.16:2-14, and following verses.

The ark was brought to Zion by David with sacrifices and merry-making, 2 Sam.6:1-19, during which Uzzah perished because he touched it, Verses 6,7 of that passage.

The ark was placed in the middle of the temple in Jerusalem, where it constituted the innermost part. 1 Kings 6:19, and following verses; 8:3-9.

Because of the Lord's presence and power within the Law residing in the ark the waters of the Jordan were parted, and for as long as the ark rested in the middle of it the people went across on dry ground. Josh.3:1-17; 4:5-20. The walls of Jericho collapsed as a result of the ark's being carried round them. Josh.6:1-20.

Dagon, the god of the Philistines, fell to ground in front of the ark, and after this lay over the threshold of the shrine severed from his head. 1 Sam.5:1-4. Several thousand people of Bethshemesh were struck down because of the ark. 1 Sam.6:19.

60   Quod tabulae lapideae super quibus Lex erat scripta dictae sint Tabulae foederis, et arca ex illis dicta sit Arca foederis, et ipsa Lex Foedus, Num.10:33; Deut.4:13,23; 5:2,3; 9:9; Jos.3:11; 1 Reg.8:9,21; Apoc.11:19; et multoties alibi. Quod Lex dicta sit Foedus, est quia foedus significat conjunctionem, quare de Domino dicitur quod erit in foedus populo, Esai.42:6; 49:8; et vocatur Angelus foederis, Mal.3:1, et sanguis Ipsius Sanguis foederis, Matt.26:28; Sach.9:11; Exod.24:4-10. Ideo Verbum dicitur Foedus Vetus et Foedus Novum. Foedera etiam fiunt amoris, amicitiae, consociationis, ita conjunctionis gratia.

61   Quod praecepta illius Legis dicta sint Decem Verba, Exod.34:28; Deut.4:13; 10:4. Ita vocantur, quia decem significant omnia, et verba significant vera, fuerunt enim plura quam decem. Quia decem significant omnia, ideo aulaea tabernaculi fuerunt decem, Exod.26:1; ideo dixit Dominus quod homo accepturus regnum vocaverit decem servos et dederit illis decem minas ad negotiandum, Luc.19:13; ideo Dominus assimilavit regnum caelorum decem virginibus, Matt.25:1; ideo describitur draco, quod haberet decem cornua, et super cornibus decem diademata, Apoc.12:3. Similiter bestia e mari ascendens, Apoc.13:1, et quoque alia bestia, Apoc.17:3,7; tum etiam bestia apud Danielem 7:7,20,24. Simile significatur per decem, Lev.26:26; Sach.8:23; et alibi. Inde sunt decimae, per quas significatur aliquid ex omnibus.

4   1 Reg.8:9,21: 1 Reg.8:19,21 VI

60 The tablets of stone which the Law was written on were called the Tablets of the Covenant, and because of them the ark was called the Ark of the Covenant, and the Law itself the Covenant, Num.10:33; Deut.4:13,23; 5:2,3; 9:9; Josh.3:11; 1 Kings 8:9,21; Rev.11:19; and many times in other places. The Law was called the Covenant because a covenant is the sign of a linking together, which explains why it is said of the Lord that He will be as a covenant for the people, Isa.42:6; 49:8, and why He is called the Angel or Messenger of the covenant, Mal.3:1, and His blood the Blood of the covenant, Matt.26:28; Zech.9:11; Exod.24:4-10. And the Word is therefore referred to as the Old Covenant and the New Covenant. Furthermore covenants are made for the sake of love, friendship, association, and so of linking together.

61 The commandments contained in that Law were referred to as The Ten Words, Exod.34:28; Deut.4:13; 10:4. They are called this because ten stands for all, and words for truths, for there were more than ten of these. Because ten stands for all, the tabernacle therefore had ten curtains, Exod.26:1; the Lord therefore said that the one who was about to receive a kingdom called ten servants and gave them ten minas to use in business, Luke 19:13; the Lord therefore likened the kingdom of heaven to ten virgins, Matt.25:1; the dragon is therefore described as having ten horns, and on the horns ten jewels, Rev.12:3, much the same as the beast rising out of the sea, Rev.13:1, also another beast, Rev.17:3,7, as well as the beast at Daniel 7:7,20,24. Ten has a similar meaning in Lev.26:26; Zech.8:23; and elsewhere. And then there are tithes or tenths, by which are meant something that comes out of the whole or all.

Quod omnis generis homicidia, adulteria, furta, falsa testimonia, cum concupiscentia ad illa, sint mala quae ut peccata fugienda sunt

62 Notum est quod Lex Sinai inscripta fuerit binis tabulis, et quod prima tabula contineat illa quae Dei sunt et altera quae hominis. Quod prima tabula contineat omnia quae Dei sunt et altera omnia quae hominis, non apparet in litera. Sed omnia in illis sunt, quare etiam vocantur Decem Verba, per quae significantur omnia vera in complexu, videatur mox supra, n.61. Sed quomodo omnia inibi sunt, non paucis potest exponi; at potest comprehendi ex illis quae in **Doctrina de Scriptura Sacra**, n.67, allata sunt, quae videantur. Inde est quod dicatur omnis generis homicidia, adulteria, furta, et falsa testimonia.

63 Invaluit religio quod nemo possit implere Legem, et Lex est non occidere, non adulterari, non furari, et non false testari. Haec Legis potest unusquisque homo civilis et moralis ex vita civili et morali implere; sed ex vita spirituali, negat illa religio. Ex quo sequitur quod illa non facere sit modo ad evitandum paenas et jacturas in mundo, et non ad evitandum paenas et jacturas postquam reliquit mundum. Inde est quod homo, apud quem invaluit supra dicta religio, cogitet illa licita coram Deo sed illicita coram mundo. Propter hanc cogitationem ex sua illa religione homo in concupiscentia est ad omnia illa mala, et solum omittit facere illa propter mundum; quare talis homo post mortem, tametsi non commiserat homicidia, adulteria, furta, et false testatus est, usque concupiscit facere illa, et quoque facit cum externum, quod in mundo habuit, ei aufertur. Omnis concupiscentia manet hominem post mortem. Ex hoc est quod tales cum

All types of murder, adultery, theft, false witness, and strong desire to do these things are forms of evil that must be shunned as sins

62 It is well known that the Law delivered at Sinai was written on two tablets, and that the first tablet contains things that relate to God and the second those that relate to people. But the fact that the first tablet includes all things relating to God and the second all relating to people is not apparent in the literal meaning of them. Nonetheless all are present within them, which also is why they are called The Ten Words, by which all truths in their entirety are meant, see immediately above, in §61. But in what way all these are present there is impossible to explain briefly, though some understanding of this may be gained by looking at what has been presented in **Teaching concerning Sacred Scripture**, §67. Here is the reason for saying all kinds of murder, adultery, theft, and false witness.

63 The idea, maintained strongly by religion, has come about that no one can fulfil the Law, even though the Law requires them not to kill, not to commit adultery, not to steal, and not to bear false witness. Anyone who is a good citizen and moral person is able to fulfil these requirements of the Law on a civic and moral level of life; but such religion denies any can do so on a spiritual level of life. As a consequence the non-doing of those things is merely to avoid punishments and deprivations in this world, and not to avoid punishments and deprivations after leaving it. So it is that people who adhere strongly to that religious idea mentioned above think that those things are allowable in the sight of God but not that of the world. Because this is the way they think, deriving from that religion which is theirs, such people are ruled by the strong desire to engage in all those evil ways yet refrain from doing so solely on account of the world around them. Therefore such people after death, although they have not been murdering, committing adultery, thieving, or bearing false witness, still have the strong desire to do those things, and actually do them when the outward shell which had been theirs in the world is removed from them. All the strong desire remains with them after death. Consequently people

inferno unum agant et non possint aliter quam sortem habere cum illis qui in inferno sunt. Sed alia sors est illis qui non volunt occidere, adulterari, furari, et false testari, quia illa facere est contra Deum. Illi post aliquam pugnam contra illa non volunt illa, ita non concupiscunt facere illa; dicunt corde suo quod sint peccata, in se infernalia et diabolica. Hi post mortem, cum externum, quod pro mundo habuerunt, illis aufertur, cum caelo unum agunt; et quia sunt in Domino, in caelum etiam veniunt.

64 Commune in omni religione est quod homo debeat explorare se, paenitentiam agere, et desistere a peccatis, et quod si non id faciat, in damnatione sit. Quod hoc sit commune in omni religione, videatur supra, n.4-8. Commune etiam est in toto Christiano orbe quod Decalogus doceatur, et quod infantes in religionem Christianam initientur per illum, est enim in omnium infantum puerorum manu. Ipsi parentes et magistri dicunt illis quod illa facere sit peccare contra Deum; imo quando cum infantibus loquuntur, nec aliud sciunt. Quis non mirari potest quod iidem, et quoque infantes cum adulti fiunt, cogitent quod non sub Lege illa sint, et quod facere illa quae istius Legis sunt non possint? Quod discant ita cogitare, num aliud potest in causa esse quam quod ament mala, et inde falsa quae favent? Hi itaque sunt qui praecepta Decalogi non faciunt religionis. Quod iidem vivant absque religione, videbitur in **Doctrina de Fide**.

65 Apud omnes gentes in universo terrarum orbe apud quas est religio, sunt similia praecepta quae in Decalogo; et omnes illi qui vivunt illa, ex religione, salvantur, at omnes qui non vivunt illa, ex religione, damnantur. Illi qui vivunt illa ex religione, post mortem instructi per angelos recipiunt vera et agnoscunt Dominum. Causa est quia fugiunt mala ut peccata, et inde in bono sunt; et bonum amat verum et ex desiderio amoris recipit illud, ut supra, n.32-41, ostensum est. Hoc intelligitur per Domini verba ad Judaeos,

Auferetur a vobis regnum Dei et dabitur genti facienti fructus. Matt.21:43:

such as these make one with hell and their lot is inevitably the same as that of those in hell. But the lot is different in the case of those who have no desire to kill, commit adultery, steal, or bear false witness, because doing those things is contrary to God. After some battling against them they have no wish, thus no strong desire, to do them. In their heart they say that those ways are sins, belonging inherently to hell and the devil. When after death the outward shell which had been theirs for life in the world is removed from them they make one with heaven; and because they abide in the Lord they also pass on into heaven.

64 Every religion shares the idea that people ought to examine themselves, repent, and cease to sin, and that if they do not they are in a state of damnation. For the fact that every religion shares this idea, see above, §§4-8. The entire Christian world also shares the idea that the Decalogue should be taught, and that this should be used to introduce young children to Christianity, since it is placed in the hands of all young and older children. Parents and teachers tell them that to do those wicked things is to sin against God; indeed when they are talking to the young children they are not aware of anything else. Can anyone fail to be amazed that these same people, including young children when they become adult, think they are not subject to that Law and that they are powerless to observe the requirements of that very Law? What reason can there be for their learning to think this way other than that they love evil ways and therefore the falsities that justify them? These therefore are people who do not make the commandments of the Decalogue religious commandments. The fact that these same people lead a life devoid of religion will be seen in **Teaching concerning Faith**.

65 Present among all nations throughout the world in which religion exists there are commandments similar to those contained in the Decalogue, and every person who is guided by their religion and obeys them in life is saved, but every person who is not guided by their religion and does not obey them in life is damned. After death, once people guided by their religion and obedient to its commandments have been taught by angels, they accept truths and show allegiance to the Lord. This they do because they shun evil deeds as sins and are therefore in a state of goodness; and goodness loves truth and love wishes to accept it, as shown above, in §§32-41. This is what is meant by these words the Lord addressed to the Jews,

The kingdom of God will be taken away from you and given to a nation bearing fruits. Matt.21:43.

Tum per haec,

Cum venerit dominus vineae, malos perdet, et vineam suam locabit aliis agricolis, qui reddent ipsi fructus in tempore suo. Matt.21:40,41.

Et per haec,

Dico vobis quod multi ab oriente et occidente venient, et a septentrione et meridie, et accumbent in regno Dei; filii vero regni ejicientur in tenebras exteriores. Matt.8:11,12; Luc.13:29.

66   Legitur apud Marcum quod quidam dives venerit ad Jesum, et interrogaverit Ipsum quid faceret ut vitam aeternam haereditario acciperet, cui dixit Jesus,

Praecepta nosti, Non maechaberis, Non occides, Non furaberis, Non eris falsus testis, Non defraudabis, Honora patrem tuum et matrem. Ille respondens dixit, Haec omnia custodivi a juventute. Jesus aspexit illum, et amavit illum. Dixit tamen, Unum tibi deest; abi, quaecunque habes, vende, et da pauperibus, ita habebis thesaurum in caelis. Veni tamen, sequere Me, tollens crucem. 10:17-22.

Dicitur quod Jesus amaverit illum, hoc quia dixit quod illa praecepta custodiverit a juventute. Sed quia tria ei deerant – quae sunt quod cor suum non removerit a divitiis, quod non pugnaverit contra concupiscentias, et quod nondum agnoverit Dominum pro Deo – ideo dixit Dominus quod venderet omnia quae haberet, per quod intelligitur quod removeret cor a divitiis; quod tolleret crucem, per quod intelligitur quod pugnaret contra concupiscentias; et quod sequeretur Ipsum, per quod intelligitur quod agnosceret Dominum pro Deo. Dominus haec ut omnia loquutus est per correspondentias, videatur **Doctrina de Scriptura Sacra**, n.17. Fugere enim mala ut peccata, nemo potest nisi agnoscat Dominum et Ipsum adeat, et nisi pugnet contra mala et sic removeat concupiscentias. Sed de his plura, in articulo de pugnis contra mala.

Also by these words,

When the master of the vineyard comes he will destroy the bad tenants and let out his vineyard to other vine dressers who will render him the fruits in their season. Matt.21:40,41.

And by these,

I say to you that many will come from the east and the west, and from the north and the south, and will recline in the kingdom of God. But the sons of the kingdom will be cast out into the outer darkness. Matt.8:11,12; Luke 13:29.

66 We read in Mark that a certain rich man came to Jesus and asked Him what he had to do to inherit eternal life. Jesus said to him,

You know the commandments, You shall not commit adultery, You shall not kill, You shall not steal, You shall not be a false witness, You shall not defraud, Honour your father and mother. In reply he said, All these I have kept from my youth. Jesus looked at him, and loved him. Nevertheless He said to him, One thing is missing in you; go away, sell whatever you have and give to the poor, and in so doing you will have treasure in heaven. Then come, take up the cross and follow Me. 10:17-22.

Why it says that Jesus loved him is because of his having said he had kept those commandments from his youth. However, three things to be done were missing in him – he did not free his heart from riches, he did not battle against strong desires, and did not yet accept the Lord as God. This was why the Lord told him to sell all that he had, meaning that he should free his heart from riches; that he should take up the cross, meaning that he should battle against strong desires; and that he should follow Him, meaning that he should accept the Lord as God. The Lord was using correspondences when, as with all His utterances, He said these things, see **Teaching concerning Sacred Scripture**, §17. For none are able to shun evil deeds as sins unless they accept the Lord and go to Him, and unless they battle against evil ways and in so doing banish strong desires. But more regarding these matters will appear in the section concerning the battles against evil ways. [2]

Quod quantum quis omnis generis homicidia ut peccata fugit, tantum amorem erga proximum habeat

67   Per omnis generis homicidia intelliguntur etiam omnis generis inimicitiae, odia, et vindictae, quae spirant necem, in illis enim latet homicidium, sicut ignis in ligno sub cinere; ignis infernalis nec aliud est. Ex eo est quod dicatur ardescere odio et flagrare vindicta; haec sunt homicidia in naturali sensu. Per homicidia autem in spirituali sensu intelliguntur omnes modi occidendi et perdendi animas hominum, qui sunt varii et multiplices. Per homicidium autem in supremo sensu intelligitur odio habere Dominum. Haec tria genera homicidiorum unum faciunt et cohaerent, nam qui vult necem corporis hominis in mundo, is vult necem animae ejus post mortem; et vult necem Domini, flagrat enim ira contra Ipsum et vult nomen Ipsius exstinguere.

68   Haec homicidiorum genera latent intus apud hominem ex nativate, sed ille usque ab infantia discit obvelare illa civilitate et moralitate, in quibus debet esse cum hominibus mundi; et quantum honorem aut lucrum amat, custodit ne appareant. Hoc fit externum hominis, cum illa sunt internum ejus; talis homo est in se. Nunc quia externum deponit cum corpore cum moritur et retinet internum, patet qualis diabolus foret nisi reformaretur.

69   Quoniam supra dicta homicidiorum genera latent intus apud hominem ex nativitate, ut dictum est, et simul omnis generis furta, et omnis generis falsa testimonia, cum concupiscentiis ad illa, de quibus infra dicendum est, patet quod nisi Dominus proviserit media reformationis, homo non posset non in aeternum perire. Media reformationis quae

To the extent people shun as sins all types of murder, they possess a love of their neighbour

67   Also meant by all types of murder are all forms of enmity, hatred, and revenge, which manifest themselves in the desire to do to death, for murder lies concealed in those bad feelings, like fire in wood beneath ash; hellfire is nothing else. This is where the expressions burning with hatred and a flaming desire for revenge come from. These are the kinds of murder that are meant in the natural sense. But in the spiritual sense all the many and various methods used to slay and destroy people's souls are meant by murders. In the highest sense however murder means hating the Lord. These three types of murder go together as one and are inseparable, for those who wish to do to death the body of someone in this world wish to do the same to that person's soul after death; and they wish to do the Lord to death, because they are ablaze with anger directed against Him and wish to obliterate His name.

68   These types of murder lie hidden within people from when they were born, but even so they learn from the time they were young children to conceal those feelings beneath the polite and proper ways to behave required of them when among people in the world. And to the extent they are in love with holding an important position or with making money they are on their guard to prevent any manifestation of those feelings. This is what people's outward demeanour is made to be when those desires compose their inward character; it is what people are like left to themselves. Now because people lay aside their outward demeanour along with the body when they die but retain their inward character it is plain what kind of devils they would be if they did not undergo amendment of life.

69   Since the types of murder mentioned above lie hidden within people from when they were born, as has been said, and at the same time all kinds of theft and all kinds of false witness, together with strong desires to do these things, which are to be discussed below, it is plain that, unless the Lord had provided the means that lead to amendment of life, people could not avoid perishing for

Dominus provisit sunt haec: quod homo nascatur in meram ignorantiam; quod recens natus teneatur in statu innocentiae externae, post paulum in statu charitatis externae, et dein in statu amicitiae externae. Sed sicut in cogitationem ex suo intellectu venit, tenetur in quodam libero agendi secundum rationem. Hic status est qui supra, n.19, descriptus est, et hic reassumendus propter sequentia, viz. –

Homo, quamdiu est in mundo, in medio est inter infernum et caelum – infra est infernum et supra est caelum – et tunc tenetur in libero convertendi se aut ad infernum aut ad caelum. Si se convertit ad infernum, avertit se a caelo; si autem convertit se ad caelum, avertit se ab inferno. Seu quod idem est: homo, quamdiu est in mundo, in medio stat inter Dominum et diabolum, ac tenetur in libero convertendi se ad unum aut ad alterum. Si se convertit ad diabolum, avertit se a Domino; si autem convertit se ad Dominum, avertit se a diabolo. Seu quod idem est: homo quamdiu in mundo est, in medio est inter malum et bonum, et tenetur in libero convertendi se aut ad unum aut ad alterum. Si se convertit ad malum, avertit se a bono; si autem convertit se ad bonum, avertit se a malo.

Haec supra, n.19; videantur etiam n.20-22, quae ibi sequuntur.
70   Nunc quia malum et bonum sunt duo opposita, prorsus sicut infernum et caelum aut sicut diabolus et Dominus, sequitur quod si homo fugit malum sicut peccatum, veniat in bonum malo oppositum. Bonum oppositum malo quod intelligitur per homicidium, est bonum amoris erga proximum.
71   Quoniam hoc bonum et illud malum sunt opposita, sequitur quod hoc removeatur per illud. Duo opposita non possunt esse una, sicut non caelum et infernum una. Si una, foret tepidum, de quo ita in Apocalypsi,

Novi quod neque frigidus sis neque calidus. Utinam frigidus esses aut calidus; sed quia tepidus es, neque frigidus neque calidus, exspuam te ex ore Meo. 3:15,16.

evermore. The means provided by the Lord for that amendment are these: people are born knowing nothing at all; early on after birth they are preserved in a state of outward innocence; then after a little while in a state of outward love of others; and following that in a state of outward friendship. But, insofar as they pass on into using their own power of understanding to think with, they are kept in a certain freedom to act according to reason. This is a state which has been described above, in §19, and that description of it needs to be repeated here for the sake of what follows –

As long as people are in this world they are living midway between hell and heaven, with hell below and heaven above, and during this time they are maintained in freedom to turn themselves in the direction of hell or in that of heaven. If they turn to face hell they turn away from heaven, but if they turn to face heaven they turn away from hell. Or what amounts to the same thing, as long as people are in the world they stand midway between the Lord and the devil, and are maintained in freedom to turn themselves to face either one or the other. If they turn to face the devil they turn away from the Lord, but if they turn to face the Lord they turn away from the devil. Or what also amounts to the same thing, as long as people are in the world they are midway between evil and good, and are maintained in freedom to turn themselves to face one or the other. If they turn to face evil they turn away from good, but if they turn to face good they turn away from evil.

This above is §19; see also §§20-22 which follow it.

70   Now because evil and good are two opposites, entirely so, as hell and heaven are or the devil and the Lord, it follows that if people shun evil as sin they pass into good, the opposite of evil. The form of good that is the opposite of the kind of evil meant by murder is the goodness of love for one's neighbour.

71   Since this form of good and that kind of evil are opposites it follows that the latter is removed by means of the former. The two opposites cannot exist together, even as heaven and hell are unable to. If they existed together they would be the lukewarm condition described in the Book of Revelation,

I know you are neither cold nor hot. Would that you were cold or hot; but because you are lukewarm, being neither cold nor hot, I will spit you out of My mouth. 3:15,16.

72 Quando homo non amplius in malo homicidii est sed in bono amoris erga proximum, tunc quicquid agit, bonum illius amoris est, consequenter est bonum opus. Homo sacerdos qui in illo bono est, quoties docet et ducit, bonum opus facit, quia ex amore salvandi animas. Persona magistratus qui in illo bono est, quoties disponit et judicat, bonum opus facit, quia ex amore consulendi patriae, societati, et concivi. Negotiator similiter; si in illo bono est, omne negotiationis ejus est bonum opus. Est in illo amor proximi; et proximus sunt patria, societas, concivis, et quoque domestici, quibus consulit cum sibi. Operarius etiam qui in illo bono est, ex illo fideliter operatur, pro aliis sicut pro se, timens damni proximi sicut sui. Quod facta illorum sint bona opera, est quia quantum quis fugit malum, tantum facit bonum, secundum communem legem, supra n.21, et qui fugit malum ut peccatum, is facit bonum non a se sed a Domino, n.18-31. Contrarium fit apud illum qui genera homicidii – quae sunt inimicitiae, odia, vindictae, et plura – non spectat ut peccata. Sive sit sacerdos, sive persona magistratus, sive negotiator, sive operarius, quicquid facit, non est bonum opus, quia omne opus ejus participat a malo quod intus in illo est. Internum enim ejus est quod producit; externum potest bonum esse, sed pro aliis, non pro ipso.

73 Dominus docet bonum amoris in Verbo multis in locis; et docet illud per reconciliationem cum proximo, apud Matthaeum,

Si obtuleris munus tuum super altare, et apud hoc recordatus fueris quod frater tuus habeat aliquid contra te, relinque ibi munus coram altari, et abi; prius reconciliare fratri, et tunc veniens offer munus tuum. Et benevolentiam ini cum adversario tuo, dum es in via cum illo, ne te tradat adversarius judici, et judex tradat te ministro, et in carcerem conjiciaris. Amen dico tibi, Non exibis donec persolveris ultimum dodrantem. 5:23-26.

72   When the evil of murder does not reside any longer in people but the goodness of love for the neighbour, then whatever deed they perform embodies the goodness of that love and is as a consequence a good work. As often as priests in whom that goodness resides are teaching and guiding people they are doing a good work, because they are acting from a desire for the salvation of souls. As often as officers of state in whom that goodness resides come to a decision and pass a judgment they are performing a good work, because they are acting from a desire to consider the interests of country, community, and fellow citizen. The same applies to those engaged in business; if that goodness resides in them every one of their business operations is a good work. Love for the neighbour resides in them, the neighbour being their country, community, fellow citizen, and domestic servants as well, whose interests they consider along with their own. Workmen too in whom that goodness resides are led by it to do a good job properly for other people's benefit as much as their own, fearing lest neighbour as much as themselves should suffer loss. The things they make are good works, for the reason that – according to the general rule stated above, in §21 – to the extent people shun what is evil they do what is good, and, in §§18-31, that those who shun what is evil as sin do what is good not from self but from the Lord. The reverse happens in the case of those who do not look upon types of murder as sins, that is, forms of enmity, hatred, vengeance, and many more. Nothing whatever they do – whether they are priests, officers of state, those engaged in business, or workmen – is a good work because every work of theirs partakes of the evil residing within them. For it is what is within them that produces every work, which may indeed be outwardly good, of benefit to others, but not to themselves.

73   The Lord's teaching in many places in the Word is about the goodness of love; and in Matthew He speaks of it as being reconciled to one's neighbour,

If you offer your gift on the altar and there remember that your brother has something against you, leave the gift there before the altar and go away; first be reconciled to your brother, and then come and offer your gift. Show goodwill towards your adversary while you are on the way with him, lest your adversary hand you over to the judge, and the judge hand you over to the officer, and you be thrown into prison. Truly, I say to you, You will not come out until you have paid off the last penny. 5:23-26.

Reconciliari fratri est fugere inimicitiam, odium, et vindictam; quod sit fugere illud ut peccatum, patet. Docet etiam Dominus apud Matthaeum,

    Omnia quaecunque volueritis ut faciant vobis homines, sic et vos facite illis; haec est Lex et Prophetae. 7:12.

Ita non malum. Et pluries alibi. Dominus quoque docet quod occidere etiam sit irasci fratri seu proximo temere, et illum inimicum habere. Matt.5:21,22.

Being reconciled to brother means shunning enmity, hatred, and vengeance, and, it is clear, shunning it as a sin. The Lord also teaches in Matthew,

All things whatever you wish people to do to you, do also to them; this is the Law and the Prophets. 7:12.

That is, do them no evil. And this is His teaching in many other places. The Lord also teaches that killing includes being angry without good cause with a brother or neighbour, and being at enmity with them. Matt.5:21,22.

Quod quantum quis omnis generis adulteria ut peccata fugit, tantum castitatem amet

74 Per adulterari in Decalogi sexto praecepto in naturali sensu non modo intelligitur scortari sed etiam obscaena facere, lasciva loqui, et spurca cogitare. Per adulterari autem in spirituali sensu intelligitur adulterare bona Verbi et falsificare vera ejus. In supremo autem sensu per adulterari intelligitur negare Divinum Domini et prophanare Verbum. Omnis generis adulteria haec sunt. Homo naturalis ex rationali lumine scire potest quod per adulterari etiam intelligatur obscaena facere, lasciva loqui, et spurca cogitare; sed non scit quod per adulterari etiam intelligatur adulterare bona Verbi et falsificare vera ejus, et adhuc minus quod intelligatur negare Divinum Domini et prophanare Verbum. Inde nec scit quod adulterium sit tantum malum ut vocari possit ipsum diabolicum, nam qui in adulterio naturali est, ille etiam in adulterio spirituali est, et vicissim. Quod ita sit, in singulari opusculo **De Conjugio** demonstrabitur. Sed illi in omnis generis adulteriis simul sunt qui adulteria ex fide et vita non faciunt peccata.

75 Quod quantum quis fugit adulterium, tantum amet conjugium seu, quod idem, quantum quis fugit lasciviam

To the extent people shun as sins all types of adultery, they love chastity [1]

74 By committing adultery in the sixth commandment of the Decalogue, in the natural sense, not only committing fornication is meant but also performing acts that are obscene, uttering things that are lewd, and entertaining thoughts that are filthy. But in the spiritual sense committing adultery means adulterating the expressions of goodness contained in the Word and falsifying the truths there. In the highest sense however committing adultery means denying the Lord's Divinity and desecrating the Word. These are what constitute all types of adultery. People on the natural level seeing things in the light of reason may be aware of the fact that committing adultery also means performing acts that are obscene, uttering things that are lewd, and entertaining thoughts that are filthy; but they are not aware that adulterating expressions of goodness contained in the Word and falsifying the truths there are also meant by committing adultery, let alone that denying the Lord's Divinity and desecrating the Word are meant. Nor consequently are they aware of the fact that adultery is an evil so great that it may be called utterly diabolic, for anyone who engages in natural adultery is involved in spiritual adultery as well, and vice versa. The truth of this will be shown in a small work on its own concerning **Marriage**.[2] But the people involved in all types of adultery simultaneously are those who in faith and life do not look upon forms of adultery as sins.

75 Why it is that people love marriage to the extent they shun adultery or, what amounts to the same thing, why they love the chastity

---

1 The words *chaste* and *chastity* relate to the married as well as single state and therefore denote the pure and undefiled rather than the virginal and celibate
2 Manuscripts found among Swedenborg's possessions after his death show that at first he not only intended but actually endeavoured to produce 'a small work concerning Marriage', before writing **Delights of Wisdom concerning Conjugial Love**, a considerably longer work, published in 1768

adulterii, tantum amet castitatem conjugii, est quia lascivia adulterii et castitas conjugii sunt duo opposite, quare quantum non in uno est, tantum in altero est. Est prorsus sicut dictum est supra, n.70.

76 Non potest quisquam scire qualis est castitas conjugii nisi qui fugit lasciviam adulterii ut peccatum. Homo scire potest in quo est sed non potest scire in quo non est. Si scit aliquid in quo non est ex descriptione aut ex cogitatione, usque non scit id aliter quam in umbra, ac inhaeret dubium; quare non illud videt in luce et absque dubio quam cum in illo est. Hoc itaque est scire, illud autem est scire et non scire. Veritas est quod lascivia adulterii et castitas conjugii inter se sint prorsus sicut infernum et caelum inter se, et quod lascivia adulterii faciat infernum apud hominem et castitas conjugii caelum apud illum. Sed non datur castitas conjugii apud alium quam qui fugit lasciviam adulterii sicut peccatum, videatur infra, n.111.

77 Ex his non ambigue concludi et videri potest num homo sit Christianus vel non, imo num homini aliqua religio sit vel non. Qui adulteria ex fide et vita non facit peccata, ille non Christianus est, nec illi religio est. Vicissim autem, qui adulteria ut peccata fugit, et magis qui propterea aversatur illa, et adhuc magis qui propterea abominatur illa, illi religio est, et si in Ecclesia Christiana est, Christianus est. Sed de his plura in opusculo **De Conjugio**; interea videantur quae in opere **De Caelo et Inferno**, n.366-386, de illis dicta sunt.

78 Quod per adulterari etiam intelligatur obscaena facere, lasciva loqui, et spurca cogitare, constat a Domini verbis apud Matthaeum,

Audivistis quod veteribus dictum sit, Non adulteraberis. Ego vero dico vobis quod si quis aspexerit mulierem alienam, ita ut concupiscat eam, jam adulterium cum illa commiserit in corde suo. 5:27,28.

of marriage to the extent they shun the wantonness of adultery, is because the wantonness of adultery and the chastity of marriage are two opposites, and therefore to the extent one does not exist in a person the other does. This is just like what has been said above, at §70.

76   None can know what the chastity of marriage is like unless they shun as sin the wantonness of adultery. People in whom it exists can know it but not those in whom it does not exist. Though people in whom something that does not exist may know of it from a description or else thought of it they nevertheless have no more than a vague knowledge of it, with doubt clinging to it. Consequently they do not see that thing in clear light and without doubt, as they would if it did exist in them. The latter therefore is knowing, the former a knowing-yet-not-knowing. The truth is that the wantonness of adultery and the chastity of marriage are completely different from each other, just as much as hell and heaven are from each other, and the wantonness of adultery constitutes hell with a person while the chastity of marriage constitutes heaven. But the chastity of marriage does not exist with any but those who shun as sin the wantonness of adultery, see §111 below.

77   These considerations help it to be deduced and seen without doubt whether someone is a Christian or not, or rather whether any religion exists in that person or not. People who in belief and life do not look upon acts of adultery as sins are not Christians and have no religion in them. On the other hand however, people who shun acts of adultery as sins, more so those who therefore keep right away from them, and more so still those who therefore loathe them, do have religion in them; and if they belong to the Christian Church they are Christians. But more on these matters will appear in the small work concerning **Marriage**; meanwhile see what has been stated regarding them in the work **Heaven and Hell**, §§366-386.

78   The fact that committing adultery also means performing acts that are obscene, uttering things that are lewd, and entertaining thoughts which are filthy is clear from the Lord's words in Matthew,

You have heard that it was said to those of old, You shall not commit adultery. But I say to you that if anyone looks at a woman[1] so that he lusts after her he has already committed adultery with her in his heart. 5:27,28.

---

1   Following the version of Sebastian Schmidt Swedenborg adds a word which implies that the woman is another man's wife

79   Quod per adulterari in spirituali sensu intelligatur adulterare bonum Verbi et falsificare verum ejus, constat ex his —

Babylon a vino scortationis suae potavit omnes gentes. Apoc.14:8.
Angelus dixit, Monstrabo tibi judicium meretricis magnae sedentis super aquis multis, cum qua scortati sunt reges terrae. Apoc.17:1,2.
Babylon ex vino furoris scortationis suae potavit omnes gentes, et reges terrae cum ea scortati sunt. Apoc.18:3.
Deus judicavit meretricem magnam, quae corrupit terram scortatione sua. Apoc.19:2.

Scortatio dicitur de Babylone, quia per Babylonem intelliguntur illi qui Divinam Domini potestatem sibi arrogant, et prophanant Verbum adulterando et falsificando illud; quare etiam Babylon vocatur, Mater scortationum et abominationum terrae, Apoc.17:5.
Simile per scortationem significatur apud Prophetas, ut apud Jeremiam,

In prophetis Hierosolymae vidi obfirmationem horrendam, adulterando et eundo in mendacio. 23:14.

Apud Ezechielem,

Duae mulieres, filiae unius matris, scortatae sunt in Aegypto; in adolescentia sua scortatae sunt. Scortata est una sub Me et dilexit amasios Assyrios propinquos. Dedit scortationes suas super illos. Attamen scortationes suas in Aegypto non deseruit. Altera corrupit amorem suum plus quam illa, et scortationes suas supra scortationes sororis. Addidit ad scortationes suas; amavit Chaldaeos. Venerunt ad illam filii Babelis ad concubitum amorum, et polluerunt eam per scortationem suam. 23:2-17.

Haec de Ecclesia Israelitica et Judaica, quae ibi sunt filiae unius matris. Per scortationes illarum intelliguntur adulterationes et falsificationes Verbi; et quia in Verbo per Aegyptum significatur scientia, per Assyriam ratiocinatio,

79 The fact that in the spiritual sense committing adultery means adulterating some expression of goodness in the Word and falsifying some truth there is clear from the following –

Babylon caused all nations to drink from the wine of her fornication. Rev.14:8.
The angel said, I will show you the judgment of the great harlot seated on many waters, with whom the kings of the earth committed fornication. Rev.17:1,2.
Babylon has caused all nations to drink from the wine of the fury of her fornication, and the kings of the earth have committed fornication with her. Rev.18:3.
God has judged the great harlot who corrupted the earth with her fornication. Rev.19:2.

The word fornication is used in reference to Babylon because by Babylon are meant those who claim as their own the Divine power which is the Lord's, and who desecrate the Word by adulterating and falsifying it. This is why Babylon is also called, Mother of fornications and earth's abominations, Rev.17:5.

Much the same is meant in the Prophets by fornication, for instance in Jeremiah, [2]

In the prophets of Jerusalem I have seen a horrible obstinacy, in their committing adultery and walking in a lie. 23:14.

In Ezekiel,

Two women, the daughters of one mother, committed fornication in Egypt; in their youth they committed fornication. One committed fornication under Me and doted on her lovers the neighbouring Assyrians. She bestowed her acts of fornication on them. But she did not give up her acts of fornication begun in Egypt. The other corrupted her love more than she, and her acts of fornication more than her sister's acts of fornication. She added to her acts of fornication; she loved the Chaldeans. The sons of Babel came to her love-bed and defiled her through their fornication. 23:2-17.

These statements refer to the Israelite and Jewish Church, which is meant in them by the daughters of one mother. Their acts of fornication mean instances of adulteration and falsification of the Word; and since in the Word knowledge is meant by Egypt, reasoning by

per Chaldaeam prophanatio veri, et per Babelem prophanatio boni, ideo dicitur quod cum illis scortatae sint. Simile dicitur de Hierosolyma, per quam significatur ecclesia quoad doctrinam, apud Ezechielem,

Hierosolyma, confisa es pulchritudini tuae, et scortata es ob famam tuam, adeo ut effuderis scortationes tuas super omnem transeuntem. Scortata es cum filiis Aegypti vicinis tuis, magnis carne, et multiplicasti scortationem tuam. Scortata es cum filiis Aschuris, cum satietas tibi nulla cum quibus scortata es. Multiplicasti scortationem tuam usque ad terram negotiationis Chaldaeam. Mulier adultera sub viro suo accipit alienos. Omnes meretricibus suis dant mercedem, tu vero dedisti mercedes omnibus amasiis, ut veniant ad te in circuitu tuo in scortationibus tuis. Quare, meretrix, audi verbum Jehovae. 16:15,26,28,29,32,33,35,seq.

Quod per Hierosolymam intelligatur ecclesia, videatur in **Doctrina de Domino**, n.62,63. Simile per scortationes significatur apud Esaiam 23:17,18; 57:3; apud Jeremiam 3:2,6,8,9; 5:1,7; 13:27; 29:23; apud Micham 1:7; apud Nahum 3:4; apud Hoseam 4:10,11; tum Lev.20:5; Num.14:33; 15:39; et alibi. Idcirco etiam gens Judaica a Domino vocata est generatio adultera, Matt.12:39; 16:4; Marc.8:38.

Assyria, the desecration of what is true by Chaldea, and the desecration of what is good by Babel, it therefore says those daughters committed fornication with these. Similar things are said in Ezekiel about Jerusalem, by which the church in respect of its teaching is meant, 3

O Jerusalem, you trusted in your beauty, and committed fornication because of your fame, to such an extent that you poured out your acts of fornication on every passer-by. You committed fornication with the sons of Egypt, your neighbours, great in flesh, and multiplied your fornication. You committed fornication with the sons of Asshur, when you were not satisfied by those with whom you committed fornication. You multiplied your fornication, even as far as the trading land of Chaldea. An adulterous woman takes strangers instead of her husband. All make a payment to their prostitutes[1], but you have made payments to all lovers, to come to you from all around for your acts of fornication. Therefore, O prostitute, hear the word of Jehovah. 16:15,26,28,29,32,33,35, and following verses.

For the meaning of Jerusalem as the church, see **Teaching concerning the Lord**, §§62,63. The like is meant by acts of fornication in Isaiah 23:17,18; 57:3; Jeremiah 3:2,6,8,9; 5:1,7; 13:27; 29:23; Micah 1:7; Nahum 3:4; Hosea 4:10,11; also Lev.20:5; Num.14:33; 15:39; and elsewhere, For the same reason also the Lord called the Jewish nation an adulterous generation, Matt.12:39; 16:4; Mark 8:38.

---

[1] Here the original Hebrew and Sebastian Schmidt's Latin translation mean – *To all prostitutes they* [ie men] *make a payment*

Quod quantum quis omnis generis furta ut peccata fugit, tantum sinceritatem amet

80 Per furari in naturali sensu non modo intelligitur furari et latrocinari sed etiam defraudare et sub aliqua specie alteri sua bona auferre. Per furari autem in spirituali sensu intelligitur deprivare alium suae fidei veris et suae charitatis bonis. In supremo vero sensu per furari intelligitur auferre Domino quae Ipsius sunt et sibi illa attribuere, ita vindicare sibi justitiam et meritum. Haec sunt omnis generis furta; et quoque unum faciunt, sicut omnis generis adulteria et omnis generis homicidia, de quibus prius. Quod unum faciant, est quia unum est in altero.

81 Malum furti intrat altius apud hominem quam aliud quoddam malum, quia conjunctum est cum astu et dolo, ac astus et dolus se insinuant usque in spiritualem hominis mentem, in qua est cogitatio ejus cum intellectu. Quod homini mens spiritualis et mens naturalis sit, infra videbitur.

82 Quod quantum quis furtum ut peccatum fugit, tantum sinceritatem amet, est quia furtum etiam est fraus, ac fraus et sinceritas sunt duo opposita; quare quantum quis non in fraude est, tantum in sinceritate est.

83 Per sinceritatem etiam intelligitur integritas, justitia, fidelitas, et rectitudo. In his homo non potest esse a se ita ut amet illa ex illis et propter illa. Sed qui fugit fraudes, astus, et dolos ut peccata, is in illis ita est non a se sed a Domino, ut supra, n.18-31, ostensum est; ita sacerdos, ita persona magistratus, ita judex, ita negotiator, ita operarius, ita omnis in suo functione et in suo opere.

84 Haec docet Verbum multis in locis, ex quibus haec sint –

To the extent people shun as sins all types of stealing, they love honesty

80   By stealing in the natural sense is meant not only stealing and committing robbery but also engaging in fraudulent dealings and, under some kind of pretence, taking other people's goods away from them. But in the spiritual sense dispossessing others of truths they believe and of forms of goodness they love is meant by stealing. In the highest sense, however, stealing means taking away from the Lord virtues that are His and attributing them to oneself, that is, claiming for oneself His righteousness and merit. These are what constitute all types of stealing; and they also go together as one, just as all types of adultery do, and all types of murder, which have been dealt with already. They go together as one because one type is present within the next.

81   The evil of stealing reaches more deeply into a person than any other sort of evil, because it is linked to trickery and deceit, and trickery and deceit worm their way right into the spiritual level of the human mind, where a person's thought and understanding reside. The fact that a person has a spiritual level of mind and a natural level will be seen below.

82   The reason why to the extent people who shun stealing as sin love honesty is that to steal is to act fraudulently, and fraudulence and honesty are two opposites. Therefore to the extent fraudulence has no place in people honesty is present there.

83   Also meant by honesty are integrity, righteousness, loyalty, and uprightness. From self, no person is able to possess these virtues in such a way that the person is led by them to love them and act for the sake of them. But a person who shuns as sins practices that involve fraudulence, trickery, and deceit possesses them, not from self but from the Lord, as shown above, in §§18-31. It is so in the case of a priest, an officer of state, a judge, someone in business, a workman, thus everyone in the office they hold and the work they do.

84   The Word teaches these things in many places, among which there are these –

Qui ambulat in justitiis et loquitur rectitudines, qui fastidit propter lucrum oppressiones, excutit manus suas ne sustineant munus, obturat aures suas ne audiant sanguines, et occludit oculos suos ne videant malum, hic in altis habitabit. Esai.33:15,16.

Jehovah, quis commorabitur in tentorio Tuo? Quis habitabit in monte sanctitatis Tuae? Qui ambulat integer et facit justitiam. Is non detrectat lingua sua, non facit socio suo malum. Ps.15:1-3,seq.
Oculi Mei erga fideles terrae, ut sedeant Mecum; ambulans in via integri hic ministrabit Mihi. Non sedebit in medio domus Meae faciens dolum, loquens mendacia non consistet coram oculis Meis. Sub auroras exscindam omnes impios terrae, ad exscindendum ex urbe omnes operantes iniquitatem. Ps.101:6-8.

Quod nisi quis interius sit sincerus, justus, fidelis, et rectus, usque sit insincerus, injustus, infidelis, et non rectus, docet Dominus his verbis,

Nisi abundaverit justitia vestra super Scribarum et Pharisaeorum, non intrabitis in regnum caelorum. Matt.5:20.

Per justitiam abundantem super Scribarum et Pharisaeorum intelligitur justitia interior, in qua est homo qui est in Domino. Quod in Domino, docet etiam Ipse apud Johannem,

Ego gloriam quam dedisti Mihi dedi illis, ut sint unum sicut Nos unum sumus, Ego in illis et Tu in Me, ut sint perfecti in unum; utque dilectio, qua dilexisti Me, in illis sit et Ego in illis. 17:22,23,26.

Ex quo patet quod perfecti sint, cum Dominus in illis. Illi sunt qui vocantur mundi corde, qui Deum videbunt, ac perfecti, sicut Pater in caelis, Matt.5:8,48.

85 Supra, n.81, dictum est quod malum furti intret altius apud hominem quam aliud quoddam malum, quia conjunctum est cum astu et dolo; ac astus et dolus se insinuant usque in spiritualem hominis mentem, in qua est cogitatio ejus cum intellectu. Quare nunc aliquid de mente hominis dicetur. Quod mens hominis sit intellectus et simul voluntas ejus, videatur supra, n.43.

    1   Qui ambulat *VI*³: Quis ambulat *VI*¹, *VI*²
    11 auroras: aurora *VI*

Those who walk in righteous ways and say things that are upright, who loathe excessive charges made for the sake of gain, wriggle their hands to prevent them holding a bribe, stop their ears from hearing of bloodshed, and shut their eyes from seeing evil, these will dwell on the heights. Isa.33:15,16.

O Jehovah, who will sojourn in Your tent? Who will dwell on Your holy mountain? Those who walk with integrity and practise righteousness. They do not disparage with their tongue, they do no evil to their neighbour. Ps.15:1-3 and following verses.

My eyes are on the faithful of the land, that they may sit with Me. Those walking in the way of integrity will serve Me. They will not sit within My house who practise deceit, those who tell lies will not continue before My eyes. Around each early morning I will cut down all the wicked of the land, to cut off from the city all workers of iniquity. Ps.101:6-8.

Unless people are inwardly honest, righteous, loyal, and upright, they remain dishonest, unrighteous, disloyal, and not upright. This is the Lord's teaching in the following words,

Unless your righteousness exceeds that of Scribes and Pharisees you will not enter the kingdom of heaven, Matt.5:20.

By righteousness exceeding that of Scribes and Pharisees is meant inward righteousness, which exists in a person who abides in the Lord. Abiding in Him is also something in His teaching, in John,

The glory which You have given to Me I have given to them that they may be one even as We are one, I in them and You in Me, that they may be made perfect in one; and that the love with which you loved Me may be in them, and I in them. 17:22,23,26.

From this it is evident that people are made perfect when the Lord is in them. They are the ones who are called the pure in heart, who will see God, and will be perfect, as their Father in heaven is, Matt.5:8,48.

85   It has been stated above, in §81, that the evil of stealing reaches more deeply into people than any other sort of evil, because it is linked up with trickery and deceit; and trickery and deceit worm their way right into the spiritual level of the human mind, where a person's thought and power of understanding reside. Therefore something will be said at this point about the human mind. Regarding the human mind's consisting of the power of understanding and together with it that of the will, see above, §43.

86 Homini est mens naturalis et mens spiritualis; mens naturalis est infra et mens spiritualis est supra. Mens naturalis est mens mundi ejus et mens spiritualis est mens caeli ejus. Mens naturalis potest vocari mens animalis, at mens spiritualis mens humana. Distinguitur etiam homo ab animali per id, quod ei mens spiritualis sit; per hanc potest in caelo esse dum in mundo. Per illam etiam est quod homo vivat post mortem.

Homo intellectu potest esse in mente spirituali et inde in caelo; sed non potest voluntate esse in mente spirituali et inde in caelo nisi fugiat mala sicut peccata. Et si non voluntate etiam ibi est, usque non est in caelo, nam voluntas trahit intellectum deorsum et facit ut ille aeque naturalis et animalis sit secum.

Homo comparari potest horto, intellectus luci, et voluntas calori. Hortus est in luce et non simul in calore tempore hyemis, at in luce et simul in calore tempore aestatis. Est itaque homo qui in sola luce intellectus, sicut hortus tempore hyemis, sed qui in luce intellectus et simul in calore voluntatis, est sicut hortus tempore aestatis. Etiam intellectus sapit ex luce spirituali, et voluntas amat ex calore spirituali, nam lux spiritualis est Divina Sapientia et calor spiritualis est Divinus Amor.

Quamdiu homo non fugit mala ut peccata, concupiscentiae malorum obstipant interiora mentis naturalis a parte voluntatis, quae sunt ibi sicut densum velum, et sicut atra nubes sub mente spirituali, et inhibent ne aperiatur. At vero ut primum homo fugit mala ut peccata, tunc Dominus e caelo influit, et aufert velum et discutit nubem, et aperit mentem spiritualem, et sic intromittit hominem in caelum.

Quamdiu concupiscentiae malorum obstipant interiora mentis naturalis, ut dictum est, tamdiu homo est in inferno; ut primum autem concupiscentiae illae a Domino discussae sunt, homo est in caelo. Tum, quamdiu concupiscentiae malorum obstipant interiora mentis naturalis, tamdiu est homo naturalis; ut primum autem concupiscentiae illae a Domino discussae sunt, est homo spiritualis. Tum, quamdiu concupiscentiae malorum obstipant interiora mentis naturalis, tamdiu homo

86   Human beings have a natural mind and a spiritual mind; the natural mind is underneath and the spiritual mind is above. The natural mind is their worldly mind and the spiritual mind is their heavenly mind. The natural mind may be termed the animal mind, but the spiritual mind the human mind. Human beings also differ from animals, in that they have a spiritual mind, enabling them to be in heaven while they are in the world. This mind is also what enables them to be alive after death.

As regards their understanding, human beings are able to be on the spiritual level of mind and therefore be in heaven, but as regards their will, they are unable to be on the spiritual level of mind and therefore be in heaven, unless they shun evil deeds as sins. And if they are not there as regards their will also, they are not as yet in heaven, because the will drags the understanding down and causes it to be just as natural and animal as it is itself.

The human being may be compared to a garden, the understanding to light, and the will to warmth. In winter the garden dwells in light but not at the same time in warmth, whereas in summer it dwells in light and at the same time in warmth. A person therefore who dwells in solely the light of the understanding is like the garden in winter, but one who dwells in the light of the understanding and at the same time in the warmth of the will is like the garden in summer. Furthermore, the understanding depends for its wisdom on spiritual light, and the will depends for its love on spiritual warmth, for spiritual light consists in Divine Wisdom and spiritual warmth in Divine Love.

For as long as a person does not shun evil deeds as sins strong desires to live in evil ways obstruct the inner parts of the natural mind on the side of the will. Those parts there are like a thick curtain and like a black cloud below the spiritual mind which prevent the opening of this. But as soon as the person shuns evil deeds as sins the Lord flows in from heaven; removing the curtain and dispersing the cloud, He opens the spiritual mind and in so doing lets the person into heaven.

For as long as strong desires to live in evil ways obstruct the inner parts of the natural mind, as has been said, people are in hell; but as soon as those strong desires have been dispersed by the Lord, people are in heaven. Also, for as long as strong desires to live in evil ways obstruct the inner parts of the natural mind, people are natural; but as soon as those strong desires have been dispersed by the Lord, people are spiritual. Again, for as long as strong desires to live in evil ways obstruct the inner parts of the natural mind, people

est animal; differt modo quod possit cogitare et loqui, etiam de talibus quae non videt oculis, quod trahit a facultate elevationis intellectus in lucem caeli. Ut primum autem concupiscentiae illae a Domino discussae sunt, homo est homo, quia tunc cogitat verum in intellectu ex bono in voluntate. Tum etiam, quamdiu concupiscentiae malorum obstipant interiora mentis naturalis, tamdiu est homo sicut hortus tempore hyemis; ut primum autem concupiscentiae illae a Domino discussae sunt, est ille sicut hortus tempore aestatis.

Conjunctio voluntatis et intellectus apud hominem intelligitur in Verbo per cor et animam, et per cor et spiritum, ut, quod amaturi sint Deum ex toto corde et ex tota anima, Matt.22:35; et quod Deus daturus sit novum cor et novum spiritum, Ezech.11:19; 36:26,27. Per cor intelligitur voluntas et ejus amor, ac per animam et per spiritum, intellectus et ejus sapientia.

are animals, the only difference being that as human beings they are able to think and talk, even about the kinds of things they do not see with their eyes, which they derive from their ability to raise the understanding into the light of heaven. But as soon as those strong desires have been dispersed by the Lord people are truly human because in their understanding they then think what is true under the influence of what is good in their will. And further still, for as long as the strong desires to live in evil ways obstruct the inner parts of the natural mind a person is like a garden in winter; but as soon as those strong desires have been dispersed by the Lord that person is like a garden in summer.

6 Will and understanding linked together in a person is meant in the Word by heart and soul, also by heart and spirit, as in the statements that people are to love God with all their heart and all their soul, Matt.22:37; and that God will give a new heart and new spirit, Ezek.11:19; 36:26,27. Heart is used to mean the will and its love, soul and spirit to mean the understanding and its wisdom.

Quod quantum quis omnis generis falsa testimonia ut peccata fugit, tantum veritatem amet

87   Per false testari in naturali sensu non modo intelligitur falsum testem agere sed etiam mentiri et diffamare. Per false testari in spirituali sensu intelligitur dicere et persuadere quod falsum sit verum, et malum sit bonum, ac vicissim. In supremo autem sensu per false testari intelligitur blasphemare Dominum et Verbum. Haec sunt false testari in triplici sensu. Quod illa unum faciant apud hominem false testantem, mendacium loquentem, et diffamantem, constare potest ex illis quae in **Doctrina de Scriptura Sacra**, de triplici sensu omnium Verbi, n.5-7,seq., et n.57, ostensa sunt.

88   Quoniam mendacium et veritas sunt duo opposita, sequitur quod quantum quis fugit mendacium ut peccatum, tantum amet veritatem.

89   Quantum quis amat veritatem, tantum vult cognoscere illam, et tantum corde afficitur cum invenit illam; nec alius venit in sapientiam. Et quantum amat facere illam, tantum sentit amaenitatem lucis in qua est veritas, Simile est cum reliquis hactenus dictis, ut cum sinceritate et justitia apud illum qui fugit omnis generis furta, cum castitate et puritate apud illum qui fugit omnis generis adulteria, et cum amore et charitate apud illum qui fugit omnis generis homicidia; et sic porro. Ille autem qui in oppositis est non scit aliquid de illis, cum tamen omne aliquid est in illis.

90   Veritas est quae intelligitur per semen in agro, de quo ita Dominus –

Exivit seminans ad seminandum; et cum seminabat, aliud cecidit super viam, quod conculcatum est, et volatilia caeli comederunt. Aliud autem cecidit super petrosa, sed cum cresceret, exarefactum

To the extent people shun as sins all types of false witness, they love that which is the truth

87   Bearing false witness in the natural sense means not only acting as a false witness but also telling lies and denigrating. Bearing false witness in the spiritual sense means telling and convincing someone that what is false is true and what is bad is good, and vice versa. In the highest sense, however, bearing false witness means speaking blasphemously about the Lord and the Word. These are the three types of meaning that bearing false witness carries. The fact that they go together as one in the case of someone bearing false witness, telling a lie, and denigrating becomes clear from what has been shown in **Teaching concerning Sacred Scripture** – at §§5-7 and subsequent paragraphs, also §57 – about the three senses of everything in the Word.

88   Since lie and truth are two opposites it follows that to the extent people shun as sin the telling of a lie they love that which is the truth.

89   To the extent people love that which is the truth, they wish to be acquainted with it, and, once they have found it, have at heart an affection for it; and none other than these arrive at a state of wisdom. And to the extent they love to do what is the truth, they are aware of the loveliness of the light that holds the truth within it. The same is so with all the other virtues spoken about previous to this, that is, the honesty and righteousness of people who shun all types of stealing, the chastity and purity of those who shun all types of adultery, the love and the kindness shown to others of those who shun all types of murder, and so on. But anyone in whom the opposites of these virtues reign does not know any aspect of them, when in fact every aspect presents itself.

90   The truth is what is meant by the seed in the field, described by the Lord as follows –

A sower went out to sow seed; and as he sowed, some fell on the path, was trampled on, and the birds of the air devoured it. Some however fell

est, quia non habebat radicem. Aliud cecidit in medium spinarum, et simul enatae spinae suffocarunt illud. Et aliud cecidit in terram bonam, et cum enatum fecit fructum multiplicem. Luc.8:5-8; Matt.13:3-8; Marc.4:3-8.

5 Seminans ibi est Dominus, et semen est Verbum Ipsius, ita veritas. Semen super via est apud illos qui veritatem non curant; semen super petrosis est apud illos qui veritatem curant sed non propter illam, ita non interius; semen in medio spinarum est apud illos qui in concupiscentiis mali
10 sunt; semen autem in terra bona est apud illos qui veritates quae in Verbo sunt ex Domino amant, et ab Ipso illas faciunt, ita fructus. Quod haec intelligantur, constat ab explicatione illorum a Domino, Matt.13:19-23,37; Marc.4:14-20; Luc.8:11-15. Ex his patet quod veritas Verbi non radicari possit apud illos
15 qui veritatem non curant, nec apud illos qui veritatem exterius et non interius amant, nec apud illos qui in concupiscentiis mali sunt, sed apud illos apud quos concupiscentiae mali a Domino discussae sunt. Apud hos radicatur semen, hoc est, veritas, in mente eorum spirituali, de qua supra, n.86 ad fin.

20 91 Communis opinio hodie est quod salvari sit credere hoc aut illud quod ecclesia docet, et quod salvari non sit facere praecepta Decalogi, quae sunt non occidere, non adulterari, non furari, non false testari, in stricto et in lato sensu, dicitur enim quod non spectentur opera sed fides a Deo; cum tamen
25 quantum quis in illis malis est, tantum non fidem habet, videatur supra, n.42-52. Consule rationem, et perspice num quis homicida, adulter, fur, et falsus testis, quamdiu in concupiscentia illorum est, possit fidem habere; tum etiam, num concupiscentia illorum possit aliter discuti quam per non
30 velle facere illa quia peccata sunt, hoc est, quia infernalia et diabolica. Quare qui opinatur quod salvari sit credere hoc aut

6   *om* non *VI*¹

on rocky parts, but when it started to grow it dried up, because it did not have a root. Some fell in the midst of thorns, and the thorns sprang up at the same time as it and choked it. And some fell on good ground, and when it had sprung up it bore fruit a hundredfold[1]. Luke 8:5-8; Matt.13:3-8; Mark 4:3-8.

The sower here is the Lord, and the seed is His Word, that is, the truth. The seed on the path is as it exists with those who do not concern themselves with the truth. The seed on rocky parts is as it exists with those who concern themselves with the truth but not for the sake of it, thus not on an inner level. The seed in the midst of thorns is as it exists with those ruled by strong desires for what is evil. But the seed on good ground is as it exists with those who from the Lord love the truths contained in the Word, and from Him practise them, that is, bear fruit. That these are the things which are meant is clear from the Lord's explanation of them in Matt.13:19-23,37; Mark 4:14-20; Luke 8:11-15. From all this it is evident that the truth of the Word cannot take root with those who do not concern themselves with truth, nor with those who love truths on an outward but not inward level, nor with those who are ruled by strong desires for what is evil, only with those whose strong desires for what is evil have been dispelled by the Lord. With these the seed, that is, the truth, takes root in their spiritual mind, a matter dealt with above, towards the end of §86.

91   It is an idea commonly adhered to at the present day that believing this or that taught by the church leads to salvation, not keeping the commandments of the Decalogue that forbid committing murder, committing adultery, stealing, and bearing false witness, in the strict and wider senses of these prohibitions. For it is said that faith received from God, not works, is what matters; yet the truth is that to the extent people are ruled by those evils, they are lacking in faith, see above, §§42-52. Let yourself be guided by reason, and see whether people who are murderers, adulterers, thieves, or false witnesses, can possess faith all the time they are governed by the strong desire to commit those evil deeds; and whether the strong desire for them can be dispelled by any other means than not wishing to commit them because they are sins, because they are the works of hell and the devil. Therefore whoever holds to the idea that believing this or that taught by the church leads to salvation, yet

---

1   The Latin here means *manifold*, but the original Greek means *a hundredfold*, which Swedenborg has in **Arcana Coelestia**, in a place where he quotes Luke 8:8

illud quod ecclesia docet, et usque talis est, ille non potest non esse stultus, secundum Domini verba apud Matthaeum 7:26. Talis ecclesia describitur ita apud Jeremiam,

Sta in porta domus Jehovae, et proclama ibi verbum hoc: Sic dixit Jehovah Zebaoth, Deus Israelis, Bonas reddite vias vestras et opera vestra. Ne confidite vobis super verbis mendacii, dicendo, Templum Jehovae, templum Jehovae, templum Jehovae, illi. Num furando, occidendo, et adulterando, et jurando per mendacium, deinde venietis et stabitis coram Me in domo hac, super qua nominatur nomen Meum, et dicetis, Erepti sumus, dum facitis abominationes illas? Num spelunca latronum facta est domus haec? Etiam Ego. ecce, vidi, dictum Jehovae. 7:2-4,9-11.

has that kind of strong desire, is nothing but a fool, according to the Lord's words at Matthew 7:26. A church of this sort is described in Jeremiah in the following way –

Stand in the gate of Jehovah's house, and proclaim there this word: Thus said Jehovah Zebaoth, the God of Israel, Make good your ways and your works. Do not trust in the words of a lie, saying, The temple of Jehovah, the temple of Jehovah, the temple of Jehovah are they. Will you steal, commit murder, commit adultery, and swear to what is a lie, and after that come and stand before Me in this house which is called by My name and say, We have been delivered – while you are doing these abominations? Has this house become a robbers' den? Even I, behold, have seen it, says Jehovah. 7:2-4,9-11.

Quod non aliquis possit fugere mala ut peccata, usque ut interius aversetur illa, nisi per pugnas contra illa

92 Quisque ex Verbo et ex doctrina e Verbo novit quod proprium hominis a nativitate sit malum, et quod inde sit quod ex innata concupiscentia amet mala et feratur in illa, ut quod velit vindicare, velit defraudare, velit diffamare, et velit adulterari, et – si non cogitat quod peccata sint, et propterea resistit illis – ea faciat quoties occasio se praebet et non fama propter honorem aut lucrum patitur. Accedit, quod homo faciat illa ex jucundo, si non religio ei sit.

93 Quoniam hoc proprium hominis primam radicem vitae ejus facit, patet qualis homo arbor foret si non illa radix exstirparetur et nova radix implantaretur. Foret arbor putris, de qua dicitur quod exscindenda et in ignem conjicienda sit, Matt.3:10; 7:19. Haec radix non removetur, et nova loco ejus inditur, nisi homo spectat mala, quae faciunt radicem, ut damna animae suae, et propterea vult abalienare illa. Sed quia sunt proprii ejus et inde jucunda, non potest id nisi invito et cum lucta, ita cum pugna.

94 Omnis qui credit quod infernum et caelum sint, et quod caelum sit felicitas aeterna ac quod infernum sit infelicitas aeterna, et qui credit quod in infernum veniant qui mala faciunt et in caelum qui bona faciunt, is pugnat. Et qui pugnat, ille ex interiori agit, et contra ipsam concupiscentiam, quae facit radicem mali; nam qui pugnat contra aliquid, is non vult illud, et concupiscere est velle. Inde patet quod radix mali non amoveatur quam per pugnam.

None are able to shun evil ways as sins, so thoroughly that inwardly they get right away from them, unless they go through conflicts against them

92   Everyone knows from the Word and from teaching drawn from the Word that from the time they were born people's own selfhood is evil, and, this being so, that because of the strong desire present from birth within them they love evil ways and are carried along into them. They have the desire to take vengeance, the desire to act fraudulently, the desire to denigrate, and the desire to commit adultery, and – if they do not think that these are sins, and do not for this reason refrain from them – they act in those ways as often as they are given the opportunity and their reputation earned for the sake of position or gain does not suffer loss. Furthermore, people take pleasure in acting in those ways if they have no religion.

93   Since people's own selfhood composes the initial root of their life it is evident what kind of a tree people would be like if that root were not extracted completely and a new root introduced. They would be like the rotten tree, which must, it says, be cut down and thrown into the fire, Matt.3:10; 7:19. The root is not removed and replaced by a new one unless people regard evil ways composing the root as ones harmful to their soul and for that reason wish to get rid of them. However since those evil ways belong to those people's selfhood and are consequently delightful to them they cannot get rid of them except with an unwillingness yet struggling to do so, thus through conflict.

94   Everyone who believes in the existence of hell and of heaven, that heaven is a state of eternal bliss while hell is one of eternal misery, and who believes that those who perform evil deeds go to hell while those who perform good ones go to heaven, is a person engaged in conflict. And a person engaged in conflict acts from an inner resolution and in opposition to the actual strong desire composing the root of evil; for a person who is engaged in conflict, opposed to something, is not intent on it, and to have a strong desire for something is to be intent on it. From this it is evident that the root of evil is removed only by means of conflict.

95 Quantum itaque quis pugnat, et sic amovet malum, tantum loco ejus succedit bonum, et ex bono tantum videt malum in facie, et tunc quod infernale sit et horrendum; et quia tale, non modo fugit illud sed etiam aversatur illud, et tandem abominatur illud.

96 Homo qui contra mala pugnat non potest non pugnare sicut a se. Nam qui non sicut a se, ille non pugnat; stat sicut automaton nihil videns et nihil agens, et continue cogitat ex malo pro illo et non contra illud. Sed usque probe sciendum est quod solus Dominus pugnet in homine contra mala, et quod modo appareat homini sicut ille pugnet ex se, et quod Dominus velit ut ita homini appareat, quoniam absque illa apparentia non existit pugna, ita nec reformatio.

97 Pugna illa non gravis est nisi illis qui omnia fraena concupiscentiis laxaverunt, et ex proposito illis indulserunt; et quoque illis qui sancta Verbi et ecclesiae in obfirmatione repudiaverunt. At reliquis non gravis est; resistant malis in intentione modo semel in septimana aut bis in mense, et percipient mutationem.

98 Vocatur Ecclesia Christiana ecclesia pugnans, et non potest pugnans dici nisi contra diabolum, ita contra mala quae ab inferno; infernum est diabolus. Tentatio, quam homo ecclesiae subit, est pugna illa.

99 De pugnis contra mala, quae sunt tentationes, multis in locis in Verbo agitur. Intelliguntur per haec Domini verba –

Dico vobis, Nisi granum tritici cadens in terram moriatur, ipsum solum manet; si vero moriatur, multum fructum fert. Joh.12:24.

Tum per haec,

Quisquis voluerit post Me venire, abrogato se ipsum, ac tollat crucem suam, et sequatur Me. Quisquis voluerit animam servare, perdet eam; qui vero perdiderit animam suam propter Me, et propter evangelium, hic servabit illam. Marc.8:34,35.

Per crucem intelligitur tentatio, ut quoque Matt.10:38; 16:24; Marc.10:21; Luc.14:27; per animam intelligitur vita proprii

95 To the extent therefore that people engage in conflict, and in so doing remove evil, goodness takes its place, and from goodness they look evil in the face and then see that it is hellish and horrid; and because that is what it is like they not only shun it but also turn right away from it, and eventually loathe it.

96 People who engage in conflict, in opposition to evil ways, inevitably engage in it as if they were doing so from self. For those who do not act as if from self are not engaged in any conflict; they stand like an automaton, seeing nothing and doing nothing, and in their thinking are being led constantly by evil to go along with it and not oppose it. But it must nevertheless be thoroughly understood that the Lord alone confronts the evil ways in people and that it only seems to those people that they are confronting them from self. It must also be understood that it is the Lord's will that this seems to them to be so, because unless it does, no conflict takes place and thus no amendment of life, either.

97 The conflict is not severe except for those who have let go of all restraints on the strong desires and have deliberately given in to them, and also for those who obstinately reject the holy things of the Word and the church. But for everyone else it is not severe. Let them take a deliberate stand against evil ways merely once a week or twice a month and they will see a change.

98 The Christian Church is called the church militant, but it cannot be described as being militant unless it opposes itself to the devil, and so to evils that come from hell, hell being the devil. Temptation, which a member of the church undergoes, is what this conflict is.

99 Conflicts against evil ways, that is, temptations, are the subject in many places in the Word. They are meant by these words spoken by the Lord,

I say to you, Unless a grain of wheat falls into the earth and dies, it remains alone; but if it dies it bears much fruit. John 12:24.

Also these spoken by Him,

Whoever desire to come after Me, let them deny themselves, and take up their cross, and follow Me. Whoever desire to save their soul will lose it; but whoever lose their soul for My sake and the gospel's will save it. Mark 8:34,35.

Cross is used to mean temptation, as it is also at Matt.10:38; 16:24; Mark 10:21; Luke 14:27. Soul is used to mean the life belonging to

hominis, ut quoque Matt.10:39; 16:25; Luc.9:24; et imprimis Joh.12:25; quae etiam est vita carnis, quae non prodest quicquam, Joh.6:63.

De pugnis contra mala, et de victoriis super illa, loquitur Dominus ad omnes Ecclesias in Apocalypsi –
Ad Ecclesiam in Epheso

Qui vincit, dabo ut comedat de arbore vitae, quae est in medio paradisi Dei. Apoc.2:7.

Ad Ecclesiam in Smyrna

Qui vicerit, non damnum patietur in morte altera. Apoc.2:11.

Ad Ecclesiam in Pergamo

Qui vincit, illi dabo ut comedat de manna abscondito; et dabo illi calculum album, et super calculo nomen novum scriptum, quod nemo novit nisi qui accipit. Apoc.2:17.

Ad Ecclesiam in Thyatiris

Qui vicerit et servaverit ad finem opera Mea, illi dabo potestatem super gentes; et stellam matutinam. Apoc.2:26,28.

Ad Ecclesiam in Sardibus

Qui vicerit, induetur vestimentis albis; et non delebo nomen ejus e libro vitae; et confitebor nomen ejus coram Patre Meo et coram angelis Ejus. Apoc.3:5.

Ad Ecclesiam in Philadelphia

Qui vicerit, eum faciam columnam in templo Dei Mei; et scribam super eum nomen Dei, et nomen urbis Dei, Novae Hierosolymae, quae descendit e caelo a Deo, et nomen Meum novum. Apoc.3:12.

Ad Ecclesiam in Laodicea

	12	abscondito: abscondita *VI*
	19-22	Qui vicerit, induetur … Ad Ecclesiam in Philadelphia *VI³*: *om VI¹, VI²*

the self in a person, as it is also at Matt.10:39; 16:25; Luke 9:24; and especially John 12:25; which life is also that of the flesh that profits nothing, at John 6:63.

Conflicts against evil ways and victories over these the Lord speaks about in the Book of Revelation to all the Churches –
To the Church in Ephesus

Those who overcome, I will grant to eat from the tree of life, which is in the middle of the paradise of God. Rev.2:7.

To the Church in Smyrna

Those who overcome, they will not suffer harm in the second death. Rev.2:11.

To the Church in Pergamum

Those who overcome, to them I will give some of the hidden manna to eat. And I will give them a small white stone, and on the small stone a new name written, which no one knows except those who receive it. Rev.2:17.

To the Church in Thyatira

Those who overcome and keep My works until the end, to them I will give power over the nations, and the morning star. Rev.2:26,28.

To the Church in Sardis

Those who overcome, they will be clad in white garments, and I will not blot out their name from the book of life; and I will confess their name before My Father and before His angels. Rev.3:5.

To the Church in Philadelphia

Those who overcome, I will make them a pillar in the temple of My God; and I will write on them the name of God and the name of the city of God, the New Jerusalem, which comes down out of heaven from God, and My new name. Rev.3:12.

To the Church in Laodicea

Qui vicerit, illi dabo ut sedeat Mecum in throno Meo. Apoc.3:21.

100   De Pugnis illis, quae sunt Tentationes, in specie actum videatur in **Doctrina Novae Hierosolymae**, Londini, anno 1758 edita, a n.187 ad 201 – unde et quales sunt, n.196,197; quomodo et quando fiunt, n.198; quid boni efficient, n.199; quod Dominus pugnet pro homine, n.200; de pugnis seu tentationibus Domini, n.201.

Those who overcome, to them I will grant to sit with Me on My throne. Rev.3:21.

100   Regarding these conflicts or temptations see the detailed treatment of the subject in §§187-201 of **The New Jerusalem and Heaven's Teaching for it,** published in London in 1758 – where they originate and what they are like, §§196-197; how and when they take place, §198; what good they bring about, §199; the Lord engages in conflict on behalf of a person, §200; the Lord's own conflicts or temptations, §201.

Quod homo debeat fugere mala ut peccata, et pugnare contra illa, sicut a se

101 Ex Divino ordine est ut homo ex libero secundum rationem agat, quoniam ex libero secundum rationem agere est ex se agere. Verum binae illae facultates, liberum et ratio, non sunt propriae hominis sed sunt Domini apud illum. Et quatenus est homo, non ei auferuntur, quoniam absque illis non potest reformari; non enim potest paenitentiam agere, non potest pugnare contra mala et dein facere fructus dignos paenitentia. Nunc quia liberum et ratio sunt homini a Domino et homo ex illis agit, sequitur quod non agat ex se sed sicut ex se.*

102 Dominus amat hominem et vult habitare apud illum; nec potest amare illum et habitare apud illum nisi recipiatur et reciproce ametur. Inde et non aliunde est conjunctio. Dominus propter illam causam dedit homini liberum et rationem – liberum cogitandi et volendi sicut a se, et rationem secundum quam. Amare aliquem et conjungi illi cui non est reciprocum, non datur; nec intrare ad aliquem et manere apud quem non est receptio. Quoniam receptio et reciprocum in homine sunt a Domino, ideo dicit Dominus,

Manete in Me et Ego in vobis. Joh.15:4.
Qui manet in Me, et Ego in illo, hic fert fructum multum. Joh.15:5.
In die illo cognoscetis quod vos in Me et Ego in vobis. Joh.14:20.

---

* [Author's footnote] Quod homini sit Liberum a Domino, videatur supra n.19,20; et in opere **De Caelo et Inferno**, n.589-596, et n.597-603. Quid Liberum, videatur in **Doctrina Novae Hierosolymae** Londini 1758 edita, n.141-149

People ought to shun evil ways as sins, and to engage in conflict against them, as if from self

101   Divine order demands that people act in freedom and according to reason, because when acting in freedom and according to reason they are doing so from self. However, these two powers of mind, freedom and reason, which people have are not their own but the Lord's residing with them. And inasmuch as they are human beings those powers are never taken away from them, because without them people are not able to undergo amendment of life; for they are not able to repent, they are not able to engage in conflict against evil ways and afterwards bring forth fruits worthy of repentance. Now because the freedom and reason people have come from the Lord and people act from these mental powers, it follows that people act not from self but as if from self.*

102   The Lord loves people and wishes to dwell with them, but He cannot love or dwell with them unless they receive Him and respond with love for Him. It is as a result of this reception and response, this alone, that any linking together comes about. This being so, the Lord has provided human beings with freedom and reason – with freedom so that they can think and wish as if from self, and with reason so that they can do so according to reason. To love and be linked to someone from whom there is no response is not possible; nor is entering into someone and abiding with someone who is unreceptive possible. Since people have the ability, provided by the Lord, to receive and respond, the Lord therefore says,

Abide in Me, and I in you. John 15:4.
Those who abide in Me, and I in them, they it is who bear much fruit. John 15:5.
On that day you will know that you are in Me and I in you. John 14:20.

---

*   [Author's footnote] That man has freedom from the Lord, see above, in §§19,20. Also in the work **Heaven and Hell**, §§589-596, and §§597-603. What freedom is can be seen in **The New Jerusalem and Heaven's Teaching for it**, published in London in 1758, in §§141-149

Quod Dominus sit in veris et in bonis quae homo recipit et sunt apud illum, etiam docet,

Si manseritis in Me, et verba Mea in vobis manserint ... Si mandata Mea servaveritis, manebitis in amore Meo. Joh.15:7,10.
Qui habet praecepta Mea et facit illa, ille amat Me, et Ego amabo illum et apud illum habitabo. Joh.14:21,23.

Ita Dominus habitat in Suo apud hominem, et homo in illis quae a Domino sunt, ita in Domino.
103 Quoniam illud reciprocum et vicissim, et inde mutuum, est apud hominem a Domino, ideo dicit Dominus quod homo paenitentiam aget; et nemo paenitentiam potest agere nisi sicut a se –

Jesus dixit, Nisi paenitentiam egeritis, omnes peribitis. Luc.13:3,5.
Jesus dixit, Appropinquavit regnum Dei; paenitentiam agite, credite evangelio. Marc.1:14,15.
Jesus dixit, Veni ad vocandum peccatores ad paenitentiam. Luc.5:32.
Jesus dixit ecclesiis, Paenitentiam agite. Apoc.2:5,16,21,22; 3;3.

Tum,

Non paenitentiam egerunt ex operibus suis. Apoc.16:11.

104 Quoniam reciprocum et vicissim, et inde mutuum, est apud hominem a Domino, ideo dicit Dominus quod homo faciet praecepta et faciet fructus –

Quid Me vocatis Domine, Domine, et non facitis quae dico? Luc.6:46-49.
Si haec scitis, beati estis si feceritis illa. Joh.13:17.
Amici Mei estis si feceritis quae mando vobis. Joh.15:14.
Qui facit et docet, hic magnus vocabitur in regno caelorum. Matt.5:19.
Omnis qui audit verba Mea et facit illa, comparabo viro prudenti. Matt.7:24.
Facite fructus dignos paenitentia. Matt.3:8.
Facite arborem bonam et fructum ejus bonum. Matt.12:33.
Regnum dabitur genti facienti fructus ejus. Matt.21:43.
Omnis arbor quae non facit fructus, exscinditur et in ignem conjicitur. Matt.7:19.

It is also the Lord's teaching that He is present in the truths and the forms of goodness that are accepted by people and remain with them,

If you abide in Me, and My words abide in you ... If you keep My commands, you will abide in My love. John 15:7,10.
Those who have My commandments and do them, they it is who love Me, and I will love them and dwell with them. John 14:21,23.

So the Lord dwells in what is His own with people, and people in those things that come from the Lord, and in that way are in the Lord.
103   Since people have that ability, provided by the Lord, to respond as well as to receive, and consequently to be in a mutual relationship with Him, the Lord therefore says people must repent; but none are able to repent unless they do so as if from self –

Jesus said, Unless you repent you will all perish. Luke 13:3,5.
Jesus said, The kingdom of God has drawn near; repent, believe in the gospel. Mark 1:14,15.
Jesus said, I have come to call sinners to repentance. Luke 5:32.
Jesus said to the churches, Repent, Rev.2:5,16,21,22; 3:3.

Also,

They did not repent of their works. Rev.16:11.

104   Since people have the ability, provided by the Lord, to respond as well as to receive and consequently to be in a mutual relationship with Him, the Lord therefore says that people must keep the commandments and bear fruit –

Why do you call Me, Lord, Lord, and do not do the things I say? Luke 6:46-49.
If you know these things, blessed are you if you do them. John 13:17.
You are My friends if you do the things I command you. John 15:14.
The one who does and teaches them will be called great in the kingdom of heaven. Matt.5:19.
Everyone who hears My words and does them I will liken to a wise man. Matt.7:24.
Bear fruits worthy of repentance. Matt.3:8.
Make the tree good and its fruit good. Matt.12:33.
The kingdom will be given to a nation bearing its fruits. Matt.21:43.
Every tree that does not bear fruit is cut down and thrown into the fire. Matt.7:19.

Et multoties alibi. Ex quibus patet quod homo faciet a se, sed ex potentia Domini, quam imploret; et hoc est facere sicut ex se.

105 Quoniam illud reciprocum et vicissim, et inde mutuum, est apud hominem a Domino, ideo homo reddet rationem operum suorum, et illi retribuetur secundum illa, nam dicit Dominus –

Venturus est Filius Hominis, et reddet unicuique secundum facta ejus. Matt.16:27.
Exibunt qui bona fecerunt in resurrectionem vitae, et qui mala fecerunt in resurrectionem judicii. Joh.5:29.
Opera illorum sequuntur cum illis. Apoc.14:13.
Judicati sunt omnes secundum opera illorum. Apoc.20:13.
Ecce venio, et merces Mea Mecum, ut dem unicuique secundum ejus opus. Apoc.22:12.

Si reciprocum non foret apud hominem, nulla imputatio esset.

106 Quoniam receptio et reciprocum sunt apud hominem, ideo ecclesia docet quod homo explorabit se, confitebitur sua peccata coram Deo, desistet ab illis, et novam vitam aget. Quod omnis ecclesia in Christiano orbe id doceat, videatur supra, n.3-8.

107 Si non receptio ab homine foret et tunc cogitatio sicut ab illo, nec aliquid dici potuisset de fide; nam fides nec est ab homine. Alioquin foret homo sicut palea in vento, et staret sicut inanimatus, ore aperto et manibus remissis exspectans influxum, nihil cogitans et nihil agens in illis quae salutis ejus sunt. Est quidem nihil agens in illis, sed usque est reagens sicut a se.

Sed haec in adhuc clariorem lucem mittentur in transactionibus de **Sapientia Angelica**.

And many times in other places in which He makes such statements. From all this it is evident that people must do these things from self, yet from the Lord's power which they must beg for; and this is to act as if from self.

105   Since people have that ability, provided by the Lord, to respond as well as to receive, and consequently be in a mutual relationship with Him, they are to render an account of their works and will be repaid according to them, for the Lord says,

The Son of Man is going to come and render to everyone according to their deeds. Matt.16:27.
They will come forth – those who have done good deeds, into the resurrection of life, and those who have done evil ones, into the resurrection of judgment. John 5:29.
Their works follow with them. Rev.14:13.
All were judged according to their works. Rev.20:13.
Behold, I am coming, and My reward with Me, to give to everyone according to their work. Rev.22:12.

If people did not have the ability to respond there could not be any imputation[1].

106   Since people have the ability to receive and respond, it is therefore the teaching of the church that people must examine themselves, confess their sins before God, refrain from them, and lead a new life. This is the teaching of every church in the Christian world, see above, §§3-8.

107   If people did not have the ability to receive and at the same time think as if from self, they could not have been told anything at all about faith; for faith does not have its origin in people, either. But for that ability people would be like chaff in the wind. They would remain motionless, as though they had no life in them, waiting with mouth open and hands hanging down for it to flow in, thinking nothing and doing nothing in things belonging to their salvation. People themselves, it is true, do nothing in those things; even so, they respond as if from self.

But all this is going to be presented in even brighter light among the subjects belonging to **Angelic Wisdom**.[2]

---

1   A theological term, for which see **Teaching of the New Jerusalem concerning the Lord**, §18
2   See – in the author's Preface to **Teaching of the New Jerusalem concerning the Lord** – the last four of the nine subjects he was intending to deal with in forthcoming publications

Quod si quis fugit mala ex quacunque alia causa quam quia peccata sunt, non fugiat illa sed modo faciat ut non appareant coram mundo

108 Dantur morales homines qui praecepta secundae tabulae Decalogi servant – non defraudant, non blasphemant, non vindicant, non adulterantur. Et qui eorum apud se confirmant quod talia sint mala, quia damna reipublicae et sic contra humanitatis leges, illi etiam charitatem, sinceritatem, justitiam, castitatem exercent. Sed si bona haec faciunt, et mala illa fugiunt solum quia mala sunt et non simul quia peccata, illi usque mere naturales sunt; et apud mere naturales radix mali manet insita et non est emota. Quare bona quae faciunt non sunt bona, quia ab ipsis.

109 Moralis naturalis homo potest apparere coram hominibus in mundo prorsus sicut moralis spiritualis homo, sed non coram angelis in caelo. Coram angelis in caelo apparet ille, si in bonis est, sicut simulachrum ex ligno, et si in veris est, sicut simulachrum ex marmore, in quibus non est vita; aliter moralis spiritualis homo. Nam moralis naturalis homo est moralis externus, et moralis spiritualis homo est moralis internus, et externum absque interno non vivit; vivit quidem, sed non vitam quae vocatur vita.

110 Concupiscentiae mali, quae faciunt interiora hominis a nativitate, non removentur nisi a solo Domino; nam Dominus influit a spirituali in naturale, homo autem ex se a naturali in spirituale, et hic influxus est contra ordinem, et non operatur in concupiscentias et removet illas sed includit illas, arctius

If people shun evil ways for any reason other than that they are sins, they do not shun them, only prevent them from becoming apparent before the world

108 Some people lead morally correct lives. They keep the commandments belonging to the second table of the Decalogue; they do not engage in fraudulent dealings, do not speak blasphemously, do not seek revenge, and do not commit adultery. And those among them who are convinced that such ways are evil for the reason that they do harm to the general public and so are contrary to the laws of humanity, are also kind, honest, righteous, and chaste in their relationships with others. But if they behave in these good ways, yet shun those that are evil only because they are evil and not at the same time because they are sins, they are still people who are merely natural; and in the case of those who are merely natural the root of evil remains in place; it has not been torn out. The good deeds they perform therefore are not good since they spring from the people themselves.

109 A person leading a morally correct life who is natural may appear before the eyes of people in the world to be exactly like someone leading a morally correct life who is spiritual, but not so before the eyes of the angels in heaven. Before the eyes of the angels in heaven that person, if concerned about things that are good, looks like an image made from wood, and, if concerned about things that are true, like an image made of marble, neither of which has any life in it; but someone leading a morally correct life who is spiritual has a different appearance. For the person leading a morally correct life who is natural is outwardly so, but someone leading a morally correct life who is spiritual is inwardly so, and that which is outward without what is inward has no life in it. It does, it is true, have life, but not that which is being referred to as life.

110 The strong desires for evil which constitute the inner impulses of people from the time they were born are removed by none but the Lord alone. This is because the Lord flows from what is spiritual into what is natural, whereas people acting from self go from natural into spiritual, and a flowing from natural into spiritual is contrary to order. This does not go to work on and remove the

et arctius sicut se confirmat. Et quia haereditarium malum sic latet inclusum, illud post mortem, dum homo fit spiritus, rumpit tegmen quo in mundo obvelatum fuit, ac erumpit sicut sanies per ulcus modo exterius sanatum.

111 Sunt variae et multiplices causae quae faciunt ut homo sit moralis in externa forma; sed si non moralis sit etiam in interna, usque tamen moralis non est. Ut pro exemplo; si quis abstinet ab adulteriis et scortationibus ex timore legis civilis et ejus paenarum; ex timore jacturae famae et inde honoris; ex timore morborum ex illis; ex timore jurgiorum domi ab uxore, et inde intranquillitatis vitae; ex timore vindictae a marito aut ab affini; ex egestate aut ex avaritia; ex imbecillitate oriunda vel ex morbo, vel ex abusu, vel ex aetate, vel ex impotentia; imo si abstineat ab illis ex lege aliqua naturali aut morali et non simul ex lege spirituali, is usque tamen interius adulter et scortator est, nihilominus enim credit quod non peccata sint, et inde illa coram Deo non illicita facit in suo spiritu, et sic in spiritu committit illa, tametsi non coram mundo in corpore. Quare post mortem, cum fit spiritus, aperte loquitur pro illis. Ex his patet quod fugere mala ut damna possit impius, at quod fugere mala ut peccata non possit nisi Christianus.

112 Simile est cum omnis generis furtis et defraudationibus, cum omnis generis homicidiis et vindictis, et cum omnis generis falsis testimoniis et mendaciis. Nemo ab illis mundari et purificari potest a se; unicuique enim concupiscentiae insunt infinita, quae homo non videt nisi sicut unum simplex, Dominus autem videt singularissima in omni serie. Verbo, homo non potest semet regenerare, hoc est, novum cor et novum spiritum in se formare, sed solus Dominus, qui est Ipse Reformator et Regenerator. Quare si homo ex sua prudentia ac intelligentia vult se novum facere, est modo sicut faciei deformi inducere fucum, ac parti interiori tabe infectae illinere smegma.

113 Idcirco dicit Dominus apud Matthaeum,

Pharisaee caece, purga prius interius poculi et patinae, ut fiat etiam exterius mundum. 23:26.

strong desires; instead it shuts them in, ever more so as it establishes itself. And because hereditary evil thus lies hidden, shut in there, when after death a person becomes a spirit it breaks through the covering which in the world had concealed it and erupts like pus through a sore that has been treated solely on the outside of it.

111 There are many different reasons which cause people to be morally correct outwardly, but if they are not so inwardly as well they are still not morally correct persons. For instance, if anyone holds back from engaging in acts of adultery and fornication out of fear of the law of the land and its penalties; or out of fear for loss of reputation and consequently of status; or out of fear of diseases that result from acting in those ways; or out of fear of quarrels at home started by the wife and consequent lack of peace there; or out of fear of a husband's vengeance or that of a relative; or if the person holds back because they are poor or else avaricious; or because they are weak owing to sickness, abuse, advancing years, or impotence; or rather if anyone holds back from adultery and fornication because of some natural or else moral law and not at the same time because of a spiritual law, they are still inwardly an adulterer and fornicator. For nonetheless they do not believe that the deeds they hold back from are sins, and therefore in spirit they consider them not to be unlawful in God's eyes; so in spirit they act in those evil ways, even though they do not do so physically before the eyes of the world. After death therefore, when they become a spirit, they speak openly in favour of them. From all this it is evident that a wicked person is able to shun evil deeds as ones that do harm, but only a Christian is able to shun them as sins.

112 It is similarly so with every kind of stealing and fraudulence, every kind of murder and revenge, and every kind of false witness and telling of lies. No one acting from self can be freed from these evil ways and be made clean; for present with every strong desire for them there are countless components which a person does not see except as the general whole. But the Lord sees the tiniest details within every strand. In short, none can regenerate themselves, that is, create a new heart and new spirit within themselves; only the Lord, who is Reformer and Regenerator, can do it for them. Therefore when people wish to be made new by using their own forethought and intelligence, it is just like applying rouge to an ugly face or like smearing a detergent over a bodily part that is inwardly wasting away.

113 This is why the Lord says in Matthew,

Blind Pharisee, cleanse first the inside of the cup and the plate, in order that the outside may be made clean also. 23:26.

Et apud Esaiam,

Lavate vos, purificate vos, et removete malitiam operum vestrorum a coram oculis Meis, cessate malum facere. Et tunc si fuerint peccata vestra sicut coccinea, sicut nix albescent, si rubra fuerint sicut purpura, sicut lana erunt. 1:16,18.

******

114   Supradictis adjicientur haec –

i   Quod charitas Christiana sit cuique, ut suam functionem fideliter agat. Sic enim, si fugit mala ut peccata, quotidie facit bona, et ipse est suus usus in communi corpore; sic etiam consulitur communi, et unicuique in particulari.
ii   Quod reliqua non sint propria charitatis opera, sed vel ejus signa, vel beneficia, vel debita.

And in Isaiah,

Wash yourselves, render yourselves pure, remove the wickedness of your doings from before My eyes, cease to do evil. And then, though your sins are like scarlet they will become as white as snow, though they are as red as crimson, they will be like wool. 1:16,18.

******

114   The following must be appended to the things stated above –

i   For everyone, Christian charity consists in them dealing faithfully in whatever their occupation may be. For then, if they are shunning evil ways as sins, they are day by day performing works that are good, and they, each one of them, have their own purpose within the whole body of the community. In addition, they are contributing to the welfare of the whole community as well as to that of each individual person.

ii   But all other activities are not strictly speaking the works of charity; rather, they are either tokens of charity, kindnesses of charity, or charitable duties.

TABLE OF
PARALLEL PASSAGES

VI	43	NJ 28-29, 32
	53	AR 529.2, VR 282
	54	AR 529.3
	67	VR 309-311
	74	VR 313-315
	80	VR 317-319